A.P. Connolly

A Thrilling Narrative of the Minnesota Massacre and the Sioux war of 1862-63

Graphic accounts of the siege of Fort Ridgely, battles of Birch Coolie, Wood Lake, Big Mound, Stony Lake, Dead Buffalo Lake and Missouri River

A.P. Connolly

A Thrilling Narrative of the Minnesota Massacre and the Sioux war of 1862-63
Graphic accounts of the siege of Fort Ridgely, battles of Birch Coolie, Wood Lake, Big Mound, Stony Lake, Dead Buffalo Lake and Missouri River

ISBN/EAN: 9783743407367

Manufactured in Europe, USA, Canada, Australia, Japa

Cover: Foto ©ninafisch / pixelio.de

Manufactured and distributed by brebook publishing software (www.brebook.com)

A.P. Connolly

A Thrilling Narrative of the Minnesota Massacre and the Sioux war of

1862-63

A THRILLING NARRATIVE

OF

THE MINNESOTA MASSACRE

AND THE

SIOUX WAR OF 1862-63

GRAPHIC ACCOUNTS OF THE

SIEGE OF FORT RIDGELY, BATTLES OF BIRCH COOLIE, WOOD
LAKE, BIG MOUND, STONY LAKE, DEAD BUFFALO
LAKE AND MISSOURI RIVER.

ILLUSTRATED.

CHICAGO:
A. P. CONNOLLY, Publisher,
PAST COMMANDER U. S. GRANT POST, NO. 28, G. A. R.
DEPARTMENT OF ILLINOIS.

DEDICATION.

Thirty-four years ago and Minnesota was in an unusual state of excitement. The great War of the Rebellion was on and many of her sons were in the Union army "at the front." In addition, the Sioux Indian outbreak occurred and troops were hurriedly sent to the frontier. Company A, Sixth Minnesota Infantry, and detachments from other companies were sent out to bury the victims of the Indians. This duty performed, they rested from their labors and in an unguarded hour, they, too, were surrounded by the victorious Indians and suffered greatly in killed and wounded at Birch Coolie, Minnesota, on September 2 and 3, 1862. The men who gave up their lives at this historic place, have been remembered by the state in the erection of a beautiful monument to their memory and the names inscribed thereon are as follows:

    John College, sergeant, Company A, Sixth Minnesota.
    Wm. Irvine, sergeant, Company A, Sixth Minnesota.
    Wm. M. Cobb, corporal, Company A, Sixth Minnesota.
    Cornelius Coyle, private, Company A, Sixth Minnesota.
    George Coulter, private, Company A, Sixth Minnesota.
    Chauncey L. King, private, Company A, Sixth Minnesota.
    Henry Rolleau, private, Company A, Sixth Minnesota.
    Wm. Russell, private, Company A, Sixth Minnesota.
    Henry Whetsler, private, Company A, Sixth Minnesota.
    Benj. S. Terry, sergeant, Company G, Sixth Minnesota.
    F. C. W. Renneken, corporal, Company G, Sixth Minnesota.
    Robert Baxter, sergeant, Mounted Rangers.
    Richard Gibbons, corporal, Mounted Rangers.

To these, knowing them all personally and well, I fraternally and reverentially inscribe this book.

INTRODUCTION.

"We are coming, Father Abraham, SIX HUNDRED THOUSAND MORE!"

This was in response to the President's appeal for men to go to the front, and the vast levies this called for made men turn pale and maidens tremble.

The Union army was being defeated, and its ranks depleted by disease and expiration of terms of service—the enemy was victorious and defiant, and foreign powers were wavering. In England aristocracy wanted a confederacy—the Commoners wanted an undivided Union. The North responded to the appeal, mothers gave up their sons, wives their husbands, maidens their lovers, and six hundred thousand "boys in blue" marched away.

In August, 1862, I enlisted to serve Uncle Sam for "three years or during the war." In January, 1865, I re-enlisted to serve another term; but the happy termination of the conflict made it unnecessary. I do not write this boastingly, but proudly. There are periods in our lives we wish to emphasize and with me this is the period in my life.

The years from 1861 to 1865—memorable for all time, I look back to now as a dream. The echo of the first gun on Sumter startled the world. Men stood aghast and buckling on the sword and shouldering the musket they marched away. Brave men from the North met brave men from the South, and, as the clash of arms resounded throughout our once happy land, the Nations of the World with bated breath watched the destinies of this Republic.

After four years of arbitration on many sanguinary

fields, we decided at Appomattox to live in harmony under one flag. The soldiers are satisfied—"the Blue and the Gray" have joined hands; but the politicians, or at least some of them, seem to be unaware that the war is over, and still drag us into the controversy.

"The Boys in Blue?" Why, that was in 1866, and this is 1896—thirty years after we had fulfilled our contract and turned over the goods; and was ever work better done?

Then we could have anything we wanted; now we are "Old Soldiers" and it is 16 to 1 against us when there is work to do. A new generation has arisen, and the men of 1861 to 1865 are out of "the swim," unless their vote is wanted. We generally vote right. We were safe to trust in "the dark days" and we can be trusted now; but Young America is in the front rank and we must submit.

The soldier was a queer "critter" and could adapt himself to any circumstance. He could cook, wash dishes, preach, pray, fight, build bridges, build railroads, scale mountains, dig wells, dig canals, edit papers, eat three square meals a day or go without and find fault; and so with this experience of years,—the eventful years of 1861 and 1865 before me, when the door is shut and I am no longer effective and cannot very well retire—to the poorhouse, have concluded to write a book. I am not so important a character as either Grant, Sherman, Sheridan or Logan; but I did my share toward making them great. I'll never have a monument erected to my memory unless I pay for it myself; but my conscience is clear, for I served more than three years in Uncle Sam's army and I have never regretted it and have no apologies to make. I did not go for pay, bounty or pension, although I got both the former when I did enlist and am living in the enjoyment of the latter now. I would not like to say how much my pension is, but it is not one hundred a month by "a large majority"—and so, I have concluded, upon the whole, to profit by a portion of my experience in the great "Sioux War" in Minnesota and Dakota in 1862 (for I campaigned both North and South) and write a book and thus "stand off" the wolf in my old age.

When peace was declared, the great armies were ordered home and the "Boys in Blue" became citizens again. The majority of us have passed over the hill-top and are going down the western slope of life, leaving our comrades by the wayside. In a few years more there will be but a corporal's guard left and "the place that knows us now will know us no more forever." The poor-house will catch some and the Soldiers' Home others; but the bread of charity can never be so sweet and palatable as is that derived from one's own earnings,—hence this little book of personal experiences and exciting events of these exciting years—1862 and 1863. In it I deal in facts and personal experiences, and the experiences of others who passed through the trying ordeal, as narrated to me. As one grows old, memory in some sense is unreliable. It cannot hold on as it once did. The recollection of the incidents of youth remains, while the more recent occurrences have often but a slender hold on our memories;—error often creeps in touching dates, but the recollections of August, 1862, and the months that followed, are indeed vivid; the impress is so indelibly graven on our memories that time has not effaced them.

The characters spoken of I knew personally, some for years; the locations were familiar to me, the buildings, homely as they appear, are correct in size and in style of architecture and some of them I helped to build. The narrative is as I would relate to you, were we at one of our "Camp Fires." It is turning back the pages of memory, but in the mental review it seems but yesterday that the sad events occurred.

A. P. CONNOLLY.

Yours truly,

A. P. Carroll

CHAPTER I.

GENERAL REMARKS—DEATH OF DR. WEISER.

Historians have written, orators have spoken and poets have sung of the heroism and bravery of the great Union army and navy that from 1861 to 1865 followed the leadership of Grant, Sherman, Sheridan, Logan, Thomas, McPherson, Farragut and Porter from Bull Run to Appomattox, and from Atlanta to the sea; and after their work was done and well done, returned to their homes to receive the plaudits of a grateful country.

More than thirty years have elapsed since these trying, melancholy times. The question that then called the volunteer army into existence has been settled, and the great commanders have gone to their rewards. We bow our heads in submission to the mandate of the King of Kings, as with sorrow and pleasure we read the grateful tributes paid to the memories of the heroes on land and on sea,—the names made illustrious by valorous achievements, and that have become household words, engraven on our memories; and we think of them as comrades who await us "on fame's eternal camping ground."

Since the war, other questions have arisen to claim our attention, and this book treats of another momentous theme. The Indian question has often, indeed too often, been uppermost in the minds of the people. We have had the World's Fair, the Four Hundredth Anniversary of the discovery of America, the recollection of which is still fresh in our memories. Now we have politics and doubtless have passed through one of the most exciting political campaigns of our day and generation; but, let us take a retrospective view, and go back thirty years; look at some of the causes leading up to the Indian war of 1862; make a campaign with me as we march over twelve hundred miles into an almost unknown land and defeat the Indians in several sanguinary battles, liberate four hundred captive women and children, try, convict and hang thirty-nine Indians for participating in the murder of thousands of unsuspecting white settlers, and if, upon our return, you are not satisfied, I hope you will in the kindness of your heart forgive me for taking you on this (at the time) perilous journey.

I will say to my comrades who campaigned solely in the South, that my experience, both North and South, leads me to believe there is no comparison. In the South we fought foemen worthy of our steel,—soldiers who were manly enough to acknowledge defeat, and magnanimous enough to respect the defeat of their opponents. Not so with the redskins. Their tactics were of the skulking kind; their object scalps, and not glory. They never acknowledged defeat, had no respect for a fallen foe, and gratified their natural propensity for blood. Meeting them in battle there was but one choice,—fight, and one result only, if unsuccessful,—certain death. They knew what the flag of truce meant (cessation of hostilities), but had not a proper respect for it. They felt safe in coming to us with this time-honored symbol of protection, because they knew we would respect it. We did not feel safe in going to them under like circumstances, because there were those among them who smothered every honorable impulse to gratify a spirit of revenge and hatred. As an illustration of this I will state, that just after the battle of the Big Mound in 1863, we met a delegation of Indians with a flag of truce, and while the interpreter was talking to them and telling them what the General desired, and some soldiers were giving them tobacco and crackers, Dr. Weiser, surgeon of the Second Minnesota Cavalry, having on his full uniform as major, tempted a villainous fellow, who thinking, from the uniform, that it was General Sibley, our commander, jumped up, and before his intention could be understood, shot him through the back, killing him instantly. Treachery of this stamp does not of course apply to all the members of all tribes and benighted people; for I suppose even in the jungles of Africa, where tribes of black men live who have never heard of a white man, we could find some endowed with human instincts, who would protect those whom the fortunes of war or exploration might cast among them. We found some Indians who were exceptions to the alleged general rule—cruel. The battles we fought were fierce, escapes miraculous, personal experiences wonderful and the liberation of the capties a bright chapter in the history of events in this exciting year.

CHAPTER II.

ST. PAUL AND MINNEAPOLIS IN 1836 AND 1896—FATHER HENNEPIN.

As St. Paul, Minnesota, is our starting point, we will pause for a little and cultivate the acquaintance of her people. The picture represents St. Paul and Minneapolis about as we suppose they were previous to 1838, and before a white man gazed upon the natural beauties of our great country. In the picture you see "one of the first families," in fact it is the first family, and a healthy, dirty-looking lot they are. They had evidently heard that a stranger had "come to town" and the neighbors came in to lend a hand in "receiving" the distinguished guest. The Indian kid on the left hand, with his hair a la Paderewski, was probably playing marbles with young Dirty-Face-Afraid-of-Soap-and-Water in the back yard, when his mother whooped for him to come. He looks mad about it. They all have on their Sunday clothes and are speculating as to whether it is best to get acquainted with the forerunner of civilization or not. Their liberties had never been abridged. The Indians came and went at will, never dreaming that the day was approaching when civilization would force them to "move on." As early as 1819 white people were in Minnesota, 'tis true, but this was when Fort St. Anthony was first garrisoned.

One of the "First Families" of St. Paul in 1835.

Anterior to this, however, a zealous Franciscan priest, Father Hennepin, ascended the Mississippi, by oar, impelled on by its beautiful scenery, and in August, 1680, he stood upon the brink of the river near where Fort Snelling now is, and erected the cross of his church and probably was the first to proclaim to the red man the glad tidings of "Peace on earth, good will to man." He pointed them to the cross as the emblem of liberty from superstition, but they in their ignorance did not heed his peaceful coming, but made him their captive, holding him thus for six months, during which time he so completely gained their confidence as to cause them to liberate him, and his name is still remembered reverentially by them.

Father Hennepin named the Falls of St. Anthony after his patron saint, and was the first white man to look upon its beauties and listen to the music of Minnehaha, as her crystal water rolled over the cliffs and went rippling through the grasses and flowers on its merry way to the bosom of the "Father of Waters."

Minnehaha, beautiful in sunshine and in shadow; in rain-shower and in snow-storm—for ages has your laughter greeted the ear of the ardent Indian lover. Here Hiawatha, outstripping all competitors in his love-race, wooed his Minnehaha and in triumph carried her away to his far-off Ojibway home. The Indians loved this spot and as they camped upon its banks and smoked the peace pipe "as a signal to the nations," dreamed only of peace and plenty. The Great Spirit was good to them; but the evil day was approaching, invisible yet, then a speck on the horizon, but the cloud grew and the "pale face" was among them. Sorrowfully they bid farewell forever to their beautiful "Laughing Water."

In these early days it was almost beyond the comprehension of man that two populous cities should spring up as have St. Paul and Minneapolis, and Pierre Parrant, the first settler at St. Paul, little dreamed that the "Twin Cities," with a population variously estimated at from 200,000 to 225,000, would greet the eye of the astonished beholder in 1896. They sprang into existence and grew apace; they met with reverses, as all cities do, but the indomitable energy of the men who started out to carve for themselves a fortune, achieved their end, and their children are now enjoying the fruits of their labor.

There is no city in America that can boast an avenue equal to Summit avenue in St. Paul, with its many beautiful residences ranging in cost from $25,000 to $350,000. Notably among these palatial homes is that of James J. Hill, the railroad king of the Northwest. His is a palace set on a hill, built in the old English style, situated on an eminence overlooking the river and the bluffs beyond. The grounds without and the art treasures within are equal to those of any home in our country, and such as are found only in homes of culture where money in plenty is always at hand to gratify every desire.

The avenue winds along the bluff, and the outlook up and down the river calls forth exclamations of delight from those who can see beauty in our natural American scenery. In the springtime, when the trees are in their fresh green garb, and budding forth, and in the autumn when the days are hazy and short, when the sere of months has painted the foliage in variegated colors, and it begins to fall, the picture as unfolded to the beholder standing on the bluffs is delighting, enchanting.

The urban and interurban facilities for transport from

city to city are the best in the world, and is the successful result of years of observation and laborious effort on the part of the honorable Thomas Lowry, the street railway magnate; and the many bridges spanning the "Father of Waters" at either end of the line give evidence of the ability of the business men of the two cities to compass anything within reason.

Minneapolis, the "flour city," noted for its broad streets and palatial homes nestling among the trees; its magnificent public library building with its well-filled shelves of book treasures; its expensive and beautiful public buildings and business blocks; its far-famed exposition building, and its great cluster of mammoth flouring mills that astonish the world, are the pride of every Minnesotian. Even the "Father of Waters" laughs as he leaps over the rocks and, winding in and out, drives this world of machinery that grinds up wheat—not by the car-load, but by the train-load, and—"Pillsbury's Best"—long since a national pride, has become a familiar international brand because it can be found in all the great marts of the world. What a transformation since 1638! Father Hennepin, no doubt, looks down from the battlements of Heaven in amazement at the change; and the poor Indians, who had been wont to roam about here, unhindered, have long since, in sorrow, fled away nearer to the setting sun; but alas! he returned and left the imprint of his aroused savage nature.

CHAPTER III.

A PATHETIC CHAPTER—CAPTAIN CHITTENDEN'S MINNEHAHA.

In August, 1862, what do we see? Homes, beautiful prairie homes of yesterday, to-day have sunken out of sight, buried in their own ashes; the wife of an early love has been overtaken and compelled to submit to the unholy passion of her cruel captor; the prattling tongues of the innocents have been silenced in sudden death, and reason dethroned. A most pathetic case was that of Charles Nelson, a Swede. The day previous, his dwelling had been burned to the ground, his daughter outraged, the head of his wife, Lela, cleft by the tomahawk, and while seeking to save himself, he saw, for a moment, his two sons, Hans and Otto, rushing through the corn-field with the Indians in swift pursuit. Returning with the troops under Colonel McPhail, and passing by the ruins of his home, he gazed about him wildly, and closing the gate of the garden, asked: "When will it be safe to return?" His reason was gone!

This pathetic scene witnessed by so many who yet live to remember it, was made a chapter entitled, "The Maniac," in a work from the pen of Mrs. Harriet E. McConkey, published soon after it occurred.

Designed by A. P. Connolly.
MINNE-HA-HA FALLS BEFORE THE WHITE MAN EVER SAW IT.

Captain Chittenden, of Colonel McPhail's command, while sitting a few days after, under the Falls of Minnehaha, embodied in verse this wonderful tragedy, giving to the world the following lines:

Minne-ha-ha, laughing water,
    Cease thy laughing now for aye,
Savage hands are red with slaughter
    Of the innocent to-day.

Ill accords thy sportive humor
    With their last despairing wail;
While thou'rt dancing in the sunbeam,
    Mangled corpses strew the vale.

Change thy note, gay Minne-ha-ha;
    Let some sadder strain prevail—
Listen, while a maniac wanderer
    Sighs to thee his woeful tale;

"Give me back my Lela's tresses,
    Let me kiss them once again!
She, who blest me with caresses
    Lies unburied on the plain!

"See yon smoke? there was my dwelling;
    That is all I have of home!
Hark! I hear their fiendish yelling,
    As I, houseless, childless, roam!

"Have they killed my Hans and Otto?
    Did they find them in the corn?
Go and tell that savage monster
    Not to slay my youngest born.

"Yonder is my new-bought reaper,
    Standing mid the ripened grain;

E'en my cow asks why I leave her
    Wand'ring, unmilked, o'er the plain.

"Soldiers, bury here my Lela;
    Place *me* also 'neath the sod;
Long we lived and wrought together—
    Let me die with her—O God!

"Faithful Fido, you they've left me,
    Can you tell me, Fido, why
God at once has thus bereft me?
    All I ask is here to die.

"O, my daughter Jennie, darling!
    Worse than death is Jennie's fate!"
*   *   *   *   *   *   *   *
Nelson, as our troops were leaving
    Turned and shut his garden gate.

Designed by A. P. Connolly.

FATHER HENNEPIN RAISED THE CROSS OF HIS CHURCH ON THE BANK OF THE MISSISSIPPI RIVER NEAR WHERE FORT SNELLING NOW STANDS IN 1618.

CHAPTER IV.

ORIGIN OF INDIANS—CAPTAIN CARVER—SITTING BULL.

There is something wonderfully interesting about the origin of the Indians. Different writers have different theories; John McIntosh, who is an interesting and very exhaustive writer on this subject, says they can date their origin back to the time of the flood, and that Magog, the second son of Japhet, is the real fountain head. Our North American Indians, however, were first heard of authentically from Father Hennepin, who so early came among them.

At a later date, about 1766, Jonathan Carver, a British subject and a captain in the army, made a visit of adventure to this almost unknown and interesting country. The Sioux were then very powerful and occupied the country about St. Anthony Falls, and west of the Mississippi, and south, taking in a portion of what now is the State of Iowa.

The country to the north and northeast was owned by the Chippewas. The Sioux then, as later, were a very warlike nation, and at the time of Captain Carver's advent among them were at war with the Chippewas, their hated foes. Captain Carver came among them as a peacemaker; his diplomacy and genial spirit prevailed, and the hatchet was buried. For these good offices, the Indians ceded to him a large tract of land, extending from the Falls of St. Anthony to the foot of Lake Pipin; thence east one hundred miles; thence north and west to the place of beginning—a most magnificent domain, truly, and which in Europe would call for nothing less than a king to supervise its destinies.

A writer, Hon. W. S. Bryant, of St. Paul, Minnesota, on this subject, says: "That at a later period, after Captain Carver's death, congress was petitioned by others than his heirs, to confirm the Indian deed, and among the papers produced in support of the claim, was a copy of an instrument purporting to have been executed at Lake Traverse, on the 17th day of February, 1821, by four Indians who called themselves chiefs and warriors of the Uandowessies—the Sioux. They declare that their fathers did grant to Captain Jonathan Carver this vast tract of land and that there is among their people a traditional record of the same. This writing is signed by Ouekien Tangah, Tashachpi Tainche, Kache Noberie and Petite Corbeau (Little Crow)." This "Petite" is undoubtedly the father of Little Crow, who figures in this narrative as the leader in the massacre.

Captain Carver's claim has never been recognized, although the instrument transferring this large tract of land to him by the Indians was in existence and in St. Paul less than twenty-five years ago. It has since been destroyed and the possessors of these valuable acres can rest themselves in peace.

In 1862 the red man's ambition was inflamed, and in his desire to repossess himself of his lost patrimony, he seeks redress of his wrongs in bloody war. Fort Snelling at the junction of the Mississippi and Minnesota rivers was the rallying point for the soldiers and we produce a picture of it as it appeared then and give something of its history from its first establishment up to date.

The great Sioux or Dakotah nation at one time embraced the Uncapapas, Assinaboines, Mandans, Crows, Winnebagoes, Osages, Kansas, Kappaws, Ottoes, Missourias, Iowas, Omahas, Poncas, Nez Perces, Arrickarees, Minnetarees, Arkansas, Tetons, Yanktons, Yanktonais, and the Pawnees. It was a most powerful nation and under favorable conditions could withstand the encroachments of our modern civilization. The Ahahaways and Unktokas are spoken of as two lost tribes. The Unktokas are said to have lived in "Wiskonsan," south of the St. Croix and were supposed to have been destroyed by the Iowas about the commencement of the present century. The Ahahaways, a branch of the Crows, lived on the Upper Missouri, but were lost—annihilated by disease, natural causes and war. The Uncapapa tribe were from the Missouri, and Sitting Bull, whose picture appears, although not an hereditary chief, was a strong man among them. He was for a time their Medicine Man and counselor. He was shrewd and a forceful diplomat; he was a pronounced hater of the whites, and has earned notoriety throughout the country as the leader of five thousand warriors, who annihilated General Custer and his command at the Little Big Horn in 1876. After the massacre, this huge Indian camp was broken up, and Bull, with more than one thousand warriors retreated into the British possessions, from whence he made frequent raids upon American soil. His band constantly suffered depletion until, in the summer of

1881, he had but one hundred and sixty followers remaining. These he surrendered to Lieutenant-Colonel Brotherton, at Fort Buford, and with them was sent as a prisoner to Fort Randall, Dakota. He was married four times, and had a large family. He was not engaged in the Sioux war of 1862, but being a chief of that nation and an important Indian character, I introduce him. He has gone to the happy hunting ground, some years since, through the treachery of the Indian police, who were sent out to capture him.

SITTING BULL,

The Chief in Command at the Custer Battle of the Little Big Horn in 1876.

CHAPTER V.

FORT SNELLING.

FROM E. D. NEILL'S RECOLLECTIONS.

On the 10th of February, 1819, John C. Calhoun, then secretary of war, issued an order for the Fifth regiment of infantry to rendezvous at Detroit, preparatory to proceeding to the Mississippi to garrison or establish military posts, and the headquarters of the regiment was directed to be at the fort to be located at the mouth of the Minnesota river.

It was not until the 17th of September that Lieutenant-Colonel Leavenworth, with a detachment of troops, reached this point. A cantonment was first established at New Hope, near Mendota, and not far from the ferry. During the winter of 1819-20, forty soldiers died from scurvy.

On the 5th of May, 1819, Colonel Leavenworth crossed the river and established a summer camp, but his relations with the Indian agent were not as harmonious as they might have been, and Colonel Josiah Snelling arrived and relieved him. On the 10th of September, the cornerstone of Fort St. Anthony was laid; the barracks at first were of logs.

During the summer of 1820 a party of Sisseton Sioux killed on the Missouri Isadore Poupon, a half-breed, and Joseph Andrews, a Canadian, two men in the employ of the fur company. As soon as the information reached the agent, Major Taliaferro, trade with the Sioux was interdicted until the guilty were surrendered. Finding that they were deprived of blankets, powder and tobacco, a council was held at Big Stone Lake, and one of the murderers, and the aged father of another, agreed to go down and surrender themselves.

On the 12th of November, escorted by friends and relatives, they approached the post. Halting for a brief period, they formed and marched in solemn procession to the center of the parade ground. In the advance was a Sisseton, bearing a British flag; next came the murderer, and the old man who had offered himself as an atonement for his son, their arms pinioned, and large wooden splinters thrust through the flesh above the elbow, indicating their contempt for pain; and in the rear followed friends chanting the death-song. After burning the British flag in front of the sentinels of the fort, they formally delivered the prisoners. The murderer was sent under guard to St. Louis, and the old man detained as a hostage.

The first white women in Minnesota were the wives of the officers of Fort St. Anthony. The first steamer to arrive at the new fort was the Virginia, commanded by Captain Crawford. The event was so notable that she was greeted by a salute from the fort.

In 1824, General Scott, on a tour of inspection, visited Fort St. Anthony, and suggested that the name be changed to Fort Snelling, in honor of Colonel Snelling, its first commander. Upon this suggestion of General Scott and for the reason assigned, the war department made the change and historic Fort Snelling took its place among the defenses of the nation; and from this date up to 1861, was garrisoned by regulars, who were quartered here to keep in check the Indians who were ever on the alert for an excuse to avenge themselves on the white settlers.

In 1861, and from that to 1866, the scene underwent a wondrous change, and volunteers instead of regulars became its occupants. All the Minnesota volunteers ren-

FORT SNELLING IN 1865.

Author's Note.

When visiting Fort Snelling during the occasion of the holding of the National Encampment of the Grand Army of the Republic in St. Paul in September, 1896, I found such a change.

The old stone quarters for the use of the rank and file during the war days were there, it is true, but are being used for purposes other than accommodating the soldiers. I found my old squad room, but the old associations were gone ; the memories of the war days crowded upon me, and I thought of the boys whose names and faces I remembered well, but they are dead and scattered over the land. Some few were there, and we went over our war history, and in the recital, recalled the names of our comrades who have been finally "mustered out" and have gone beyond the river.

The present commandant of the beautiful new fort is Colonel John H. Page of the Third United States Infantry. This officer has been continuously in the service since April, 1861. He was a private in Company A, First Illinois Artillery, and went through all the campaigning of this command until the close of the war, when he received an appointment in the Regular Establishment, and as Captain was placed on recruiting service in Chicago.

His advancement in his regiment has been phenomenal, and to be called to the command of a regiment of so renowned a record as has the Third Infantry, is an honor to any man, no matter where he won his spurs.

Colonel Page is a Comrade of U. S. Grant Post No. 28, Grand Army of the Republic, Department of Illinois, and is also a Companion of the Loyal Legion. He thas an interesting family who live with him in the enjoyment of his well-earned laurels.

MINNESOTA MASSACRE—1862. 37

dezvoused here preparatory to taking the field. Some years after the war the department determined to make this historic place one of the permanent forts, and commenced a series of improvements. Now it is one of the finest within the boundary of our country, and we find the grounds, 1,500 acres in extent, beautifully laid out, and extensive buildings with all the modern improvements erected for the accommodation of Uncle Sam's soldiers.

The present post structures consist of an executive building, 93x64 feet, of Milwaukee brick, two stories and a basement, heated by furnaces and with good water supply. It contains offices for the commanding general and department staff. The officers' quarters: a row of thirteen brick buildings with all the modern improvements, hot and cold water, and a frame stable for each building. Minnesota Row: Six double one-story frame buildings, affording twelve sets of quarters for clerks and employes. Brick Row: A two-story brick building, 123x31 feet, with cellars, having sixteen suites of two rooms each, for unmarried general service clerks and employes. Quartermaster's employes have a one-story brick building, 147x30 feet, containing eight sets of quarters of two rooms each, also a mess-house, one story brick, 58x25 feet, containing a kitchen and dining room, with cellar 30x12 feet. Engineer's quarters, school house, quartermaster's corrals, brick stables, blacksmith shops, frame carriage house, granary and hay-house, ice house, etc., good water works, sewer system, and electric lights.

CHAPTER VI.

THE ALARM.

The Indians! The Indians are coming! How the cry rang out and struck terror to the hearts of the bravest. It brought to mind the stories of early days, of this great Republic, when the east was but sparsely settled, and the great west an unknown country, with the Indian monarch of all he surveyed. The vast prairies, with their great herds of buffalo were like the trackless seas; the waving forests, dark and limitless; mountain ranges—the Alleghanies, the Rockies and the Sierra Nevadas, towering above the clouds; the countless lakes—fresh and salt, hot and cold; the great inland seas; the gigantic water falls, and the laughing waters; the immense rivers, little rivulets at the mountain source, accumulating as they flowed on in their immensity, as silently and sullenly they wend their way to the sea; the rocky glens and great canyons, the wonder of all the world. It was in the early day of our Republic, when the hardy pioneer took his little family and out in the wilderness sought a new home; a time when the Indian, jealous of the white man's encroachment, and possessor by right of previous occupation, of this limitless, rich and wonderful empire, when great and powerful Indian nations—The Delawares,

SQUAD ROOM AT FORT SNELLING.

the Hurons, the Floridas, and other tribes in their native splendor and independence, said to the pale face, "Thus far shalt thou go, and no farther." The terror-stricken people were obliged to flee to places of safety, or succumb to the tomahawk; and on throughout the Seminole, the Black Hawk and other wars, including the great Minnesota Massacre of 1862.

Reader accompany me. The atmosphere is surcharged with excitement, and the whole country is terror-stricken. The southland is drenched in blood, and the earth trembles under the tread of marching thousands.

The eyes of the nation are turned in that direction, and the whole civilized world is interested in the greatest civil war of the world's history. The levies from the states are enormous, and the stalwarts, by regiments and brigades, respond to the call for "Six Hundred Thousand more."

The loyal people of the frontier have long since ceased to look upon the Indians as enemies, and tearfully urge their husbands and sons to rally to the colors in the South. What is taking place in the land of the Dakotahs?

Their empire is fading away, their power is on the wane, their game is scarce, and they look with disgust and disfavor upon their unnatural environments. In poetry and in prose we have read of them in their natural way of living. They have been wronged; their vast empire has slipped away from them; they laugh, they scowl and run from tribe to tribe; they have put on the war-paint and broken the pipe of peace; with brandishing tomahawk and glistening scalping knife they are on the trail of the innocent.

"Turn out, the regulars are coming!" were the ringing words of Paul Revere, as he, in mad haste, on April 18,

1775, on foaming steed, rode through the lowlands of Middlesex; so, too, are the unsuspecting people in Minnesota aroused by the cry of a courier, who, riding along at a break-neck speed shouts: "The Indians, the Indians are coming!" All nature is aglow; the sun rises from his eastern bed and spreads his warm, benign rays over this prairie land, and its happy occupants, as this terrific sound rings out on the morning air, are aroused and the cry: "Come over and help us" from the affrighted families, as they forsake their homes and flee for their lives, speeds on its way to ears that listen and heed their earnest, heart-piercing not, of despair, for the "Boys in Blue" respond.

The people had been warned by friendly Indians that the fire brands would soon be applied; and that once started, none could tell where it would end. They were implored to take heed and prepare for the worst; but unsuspecting, they had been so long among their Indian friends, they could not believe that treachery would bury all feelings of friendship; but alas! thousands were slain.

Go with me into their country and witness the sad results of a misguided people, and note how there was a division in their camp. The hot young bloods, ever ready for adventure and bloody adventure at that, had dragged their nation into an unnecessary war and the older men and conservative men with sorrowful hearts counselled together how best to extricate themselves and protect the lives of those who were prisoners among them. The campaign of 1862 is on.

CHAPTER VII.

SOME OF THE CAUSES OF THE WAR.

Lo! the poor Indian, has absorbed much of the people's attention and vast sums of Uncle Sam's money; and being a participant in the great Sioux war of 1862, what I write deals with facts and not fiction, as we progress from Fort Snelling, Minnesota, to "Camp Release," where we found and released over four hundred white captives. But I will digress for a time and look into the causes leading up to this cruel Sioux war that cost so many lives and so much treasure. There is a great diversity of opinion on this question, and while not particularly in love with the Indian, I have not the temerity to criticise the Almighty because he puts his impress white upon some, and red upon others; neither shall I sit in judgment and say there are no good Indians—except dead ones. The Indian question proper is of too great a magnitude to analyze and treat with intelligence in this little book; but in the abstract, and before we enter upon the active campaign against them, let us look at it and see if the blame does not to a great extent rest more with the government than it does with these people. The Indians came from we know not where—legends have been written and tradition mentions them as among the earliest known possessors of this great western world. The biologist speculates, and it is a matter of grave doubt as to their origin. Certain it is, that as far back as the time of Columbus they were found here, and we read nothing in the early history of the voyages of this wonderful navigator to convince us that the Indians were treacherous;—indeed we would rather incline to the opposite opinion. The racial war began with the conquest of the Spaniards. In their primitive condition, the Indians were possessed of a harmless superstition—they knew no one but of their kind; knew nothing of another world; knew nothing of any other continent in this world. When they discovered the white men and the ships with their sails spread, they looked upon the former as supernatural beings and the ships as great monsters with wings. Civilization and the Indian nature are incompatible and evidences of this were soon apparent. The ways of the Europeans were of course unknown to them. They were innocent of the white man's avaricious propensities and the practice of "give and take" (and generally more take than give) was early inaugurated by the sailors of Columbus and the nefarious practice has been played by a certain class of Americans ever since. Soon their suspicions were aroused and friendly intercourse gave place to wars of extermination. The Indian began to look upon the white man as his natural enemy; fighting ensued; tribes became extinct; territory was ceded, and abandoned. Soon after American Independence had been declared, the Indians became the wards of the nation. The government, instead of treating them as wards and children, has uniformly allowed them to settle their own disputes in their own peculiar and savage way, and has looked upon the bloody feuds among the different tribes much as Plug

Uglies and Thugs do a disreputable slugging match or dog-fight. A writer says:

"If they are wards of the nation, why not take them under the strong arm of the law and deal with them as with others who break the law? Make an effort to civilize, and if civilization exterminates them it will be an honorable death,—to the nation at least. Send missionaries among them instead of thieving traders; implements of peace, rather than weapons of war; Bibles instead of scalping knives; religious tracts instead of war paint; make an effort to Christianize instead of encouraging them in their savagery and laziness; such a course would receive the commendation and acquiescence of the Christian world."

There is not a sensible, unprejudiced man in America to-day, who gives the matter thought, but knows that the broken treaties and dishonest dealing with the Indians are a disgrace to this nation; and the impress of injustice is deeply and justly engraven upon the savage mind. The lesson taught by observation was that lying was no disgrace, adultery no sin, and theft no crime. This they learned from educated white men who had been sent to them as the representatives of the government; and these educated gentlemen (?) looked upon the Indian as common property, and to filch him of his money by dishonest practices, a pleasant pastime. The Indian woman did not escape his lecherous eye and if his base proposals were rejected, he had other means to resort to to enable him to accomplish his base desire. These wards were only Indians and why respect their feelings? "Sow the wind and reap the whirlwind." The whirlwind came and oh, the sad results!

The Indians were circumscribed in their hunting grounds by the onward march of civilization which crowded them on every side and their only possible hope from starvation, was in the fidelity with which a great nation kept its pledges. 'Tis true, money was appropriated by the government for this purpose, but it is equally true that gamblers and thieving traders set up fictitious claims and the Indians came out in debt and their poor families were left to starve. Hungry, exasperated and utterly powerless to help themselves, they resolved on savage vengeance when the propitious time arrived.

"The villainy you teach me I will execute," became a living, bloody issue. This did not apply alone to the Sioux nation, but to the Chippewas as well. These people have always been friends of the whites, and have uniformly counselled peace; but broken pledges and impositions filled the friendly ones with sorrow, and the others with anger. The commissioners, no doubt, rectified the wrong as soon as it was brought to their notice, but the Indians were plucked all the same and had sense enough to know it. Our country is cursed with politicians—the statesmen seem to have disappeared; but, the politician grows like rank weeds and the desire for "boodle" permeates our municipal, state and national affairs. Our Indian system has presented a fat field so long as these wards of the nation submitted to being fleeced by unprincipled agents and their gambling friends, but at last, the poor Indian is aroused to the enormity of the imposition and the innocent whites had to suffer. In some instances the vengeance of God followed the unscrupulous agent and the scalping knife in the hand of the injured Indian was made the instrument whereby this retribution came.

There has been a great deal said of Indian warriors— we have read of them in poetry and in prose and of the beautiful Indian maiden as well. The Sioux warriors are tall, athletic, fine looking men, and those who have not been degraded by the earlier and rougher frontier white man, or had their intellects destroyed by the white man's fire-water, possess minds of a high order and can reason with a correctness that would astonish our best scholars and put to blush many of our so-called statesmen, and entirely put to rout a majority of the men who, by the grace of men's votes hold down Congressional chairs. Yet they are called savages and are associated in our minds with tomahawks and scalping knives. Few regard them as reasoning creatures and some even think they are not endowed by their Creator with souls. Good men are sending Bibles to all parts of the world, sermons are preached in behalf of our fellow-creatures who are perishing in regions known only to us by name; yet here within easy reach, but a few miles from civilization, surrounded by churches and schools and all the moral influences abounding in Christian society; here, in a country endowed with every advantage that God can bestow, are perishing, body and soul, our countrymen—perishing from disease, starvation and intemperance and all the evils incident to their unhappy condition. I have no apology to make for the savage atrocities of any people, be they heathen or Christian, or pretended Christian; and we can point to pages of history where the outrages perpetrated by the soldiers of so-called Christian nations, under the sanction of their governments, would cause the angels to weep. Look at bleeding Armenia, the victim of the lecherous Turk, who has satiated his brutal, bestial nature in the blood and innocency of tens of thousands of men, women and children; and yet, the Christian nations of the world look on with indifference at these atrocities and pray: "Oh, Lord, pour out Thy blessings on us and protect us while we are unmindful of the appeals of mothers and daughters in poor Armenia!"

This royal, lecherous, murderous Turk, instead of being dethroned and held to a strict accountability for the horrible butcheries, and worse than butcheries, going on within his kingdom and for which he, and he alone, is responsible, is held in place by Christian and civilized nations for fear that some one shall, in the partition of his unholy empire, get a bigger slice than is its equitable share.

The "sick man" has been allowed for the last half century to commit the most outrageous crimes against an inoffensive, honest, progressive, and law-abiding people, and no vigorous protest has gone out against it. Shall we, then, mercilessly condemn the poor Indians because, driven from pillar to post, with the government pushing in front and hostile tribes and starvation in their rear, they have in vain striven for a bare existence? Whole families have starved while the fathers were away on their hunt for game. Through hunger and disease powerful tribes have become but a mere band of vagabonds.

America, as she listens to the dying wail of the red man, driven from the forests of his childhood and the graves of his fathers, cannot afford to throw stones; but rather let her redeem her broken pledges to these helpless, benighted, savage children, and grant them the protection they have the right to expect, nay, demand.

"I will wash my hands in innocency" will not suffice. Let the government make amends, and in the future mete out to the dishonest agent such a measure of punishment as will strike terror to him and restore the confidence of the Indians who think they have been unjustly dealt with. But to my theme.

The year of which I write was a time in St. Paul when the Indian was almost one's next door neighbor,—a time when trading between St. Paul and Winnipeg was carried on principally by half-breeds, and the mode of transportation the crude Red river cart, which is made entirely of wood,—not a scrap of iron in its whole make-up. The team they used was one ox to a cart, and the creak of this long half-breed train, as it wended its way over the trackless country, could be heard twice a year as it came down to the settlements laden with furs to exchange for supplies for families, and hunting purposes. It was at a time when the hostile bands of Sioux met bands of Chippewas, and in the immediate vicinity engaged in deadly conflict, while little attention was paid to their feuds by the whites or the government at Washington.

CHAPTER VIII.

LITTLE CROW AT DEVIL'S LAKE.

It was in August, 1861, on the western border of Devil's Lake, Dakota, there sat an old Indian chief in the shade of his wigwam, preparing a fresh supply of kinnikinnick.

The mantle of evening was veiling the sky as this old chief worked and the events of the past were crowding his memory. He muses alone at the close of the day, while the wild bird skims away on its homeward course and the gathering gloom of eventide causes a sigh to escape his breast, as many sweet pictures of past happy years "come flitting again with their hopes and their fears." The embers of the fire have gone out and he and his dog alone are resting on the banks of the lake after the day's hunt; and, as he muses, he wanders back to the time when in legend lore the Indian owned the Western world; the hills and the valleys, the vast plains and their abundance, the rivers, the lakes and the mountains were his; great herds of buffalo wended their way undisturbed by the white hunter; on every hand abundance met his gaze, and the proud Red Man with untainted blood, and an eye filled with fire, looked out toward the four points of the compass, and, with beating heart, thanked the Great Spirit for this goodly heritage. To disturb his dream the white

Designed by A. P. Connolly.

LITTLE CROW SITTING MEDITATING ON THE BANKS OF DEVIL'S LAKE, DAKOTA, AUGUST, 1862.

man came, and as the years rolled on, step by step, pressed him back;—civilization brought its cunning and greed for money-getting. A generous government, perhaps too confiding, allowed unprincipled men to rob and crowd, and crowd and rob, until the Mississippi is reached and the farther West is portioned out to him for his future residence. The influx of whites from Europe and the rapidly increasing population demand more room, and another move is planned by the government for the Indians, until they are crowding upon the borders of unfriendly tribes.

This old chief of whom we speak awoke from his meditative dream, and in imagination we see him with shaded eyes looking afar off toward the mountain. He beholds a cloud no bigger than a man's hand; he strains his eye, and eagerly looks, for he sees within the pent-up environments of this cloud all the hatred and revenge with which his savage race is endowed. The cloud that is gathering is not an imaginative one, but it will burst in time upon the heads of guilty and innocent alike; and the old chief chuckles as he thinks of the scalps he will take from the hated whites, and the great renown, and wonderful power yet in store for him. His runners go out visiting other bands and tell what the old chief expects. They give their assent to it, and as they talk and speculate, they too, become imbued with a spirit of revenge and a desire to gain back the rich heritage their fathers once held in possession for them, but which has passed from their control. They are not educated, it is true, but nature has endowed them with intelligence enough to understand that their fathers had bartered away an empire, and in exchange had taken a limited country, illy adapted to their wants and crude, uncivilized habits. This old chief's mind is made up, and we will meet him again—aye! on fields of blood and carnage.

The government had acted in good faith, and had supplied the Indians with material for building small brick houses, furnishing, in addition to money payments and clothing, farming implements and all things necessary to enable them to support themselves on their fertile farms; and missionaries, also, were among them, and competent teachers, ready to give the young people, as they grew up, an education, to enable them to better their condition and take on the habits and language of the white settlers.

But the devil among the Indians, as among the whites, finds "some mischief still for idle hands to do;" gamblers and other unprincipled men followed the agents, hobnobbed with them, and laid their plans to "hold-up and bunko" the Indians, who, filled with fire-water and a passion for gambling, soon found themselves stripped of money, ponies and blankets, with nothing in view but a long, cold, dreary winter and starvation. A gambler could kill an Indian and all he had to fear was an Indian's vengeance (for the civil law never took cognizance of the crime); but if an Indian, filled with rum, remorse and revenge, killed a gambler, he was punished to the full extent of the law. In this one thing the injustice was so apparent that even an Indian could see it; and he made up his mind that when the time came he would even up the account. The savage Indians were intelligent enough to know that in these transactions it was the old story of the handle on the jug—all on one side.

Those of the "friendlies" who were Christianized and civilized were anxious to bury forever all remains of savagery and become citizens of the nation, and if the government had placed honorable men over them to administer the law, their influence would have been felt, and in time the leaven of law and order, would have leavened the whole Sioux nation. The various treaties that had been made with them by the government did not seem to satisfy the majority, and whether there was any just cause for this dissatisfaction I do not propose to discuss; but, that a hostile feeling did exist was apparent, as subsequent events proved.

The provisions of the treaties for periodical money payments, although carried out with substantial honesty, failed to fulfill the exaggerated expectations of the Indians; and these matters of irritation added fuel to the fire of hostility, which always has, and always will exist between a civilized and a barbarous nation, when brought into immediate contact; and especially has this been the case where the savages were proud, brave and lordly warriors, who looked with supreme contempt upon all civilized methods of obtaining a living, and who felt amply able to defend themselves and avenge their wrongs. Nothing special has been discovered to have taken place other than the general dissatisfaction referred to, to which the outbreak of 1862 can be immediately attributed. This outbreak was charged to emissaries from the Confederates of the South, but there was no foundation for these allegations. The main reason was that the Indians were hungry and angry; they had become restless, and busy-bodies among them had instilled within them the idea that the great war in the South was drawing off able-bodied men and leaving the women and children at home helpless. Some of the ambitious chiefs thought it a good opportunity to regain their lost country and exalt themselves in the eyes of their people. The most ambitious of the lot was Little Crow, the old chief we saw sitting in the shade of his wigwam on Devil's Lake. He was a wily old fox and knew how to enlist the braves on his side. After the battles of Birch Coolie and Wood Lake, Minnesota, in September, 1862, he deserted his warriors, and was discovered one day down in the settlements picking berries upon which to subsist. Refusing to surrender, he was shot, and in his death the whites were relieved of an implacable foe, and the Indians deprived of an intrepid and daring leader.

There was nothing about the agencies up to August 18, 1862, to indicate that the Indians intended, or even thought, of an attack. Everything had an appearance of quiet and security. On the 17th of August, however, a small party of Indians appeared at Acton, Minnesota, and murdered several settlers, but it was not generally thought that they left the agency with this in mind; this killing was an afterthought, a diversion; but, on the news of these murders reaching the Indians at the Upper Agency on the 18th, open hostilities were at once commenced and the whites and traders indiscriminately murdered. George Spencer was the only white man in the stores who escaped with his life. He was twice wounded, however, and running upstairs in the loft hid himself away and remained concealed until the Indians, thinking no more white people remained, left the place, when an old squaw took Spencer to her home and kept him until his fast friend, Shaska, came and took him under his protection. The picture of Spencer is taken from an old-time photograph.

The missionaries residing a short distance above the

Yellow Medicine, and their people, with a few others, were notified by friendly disposed Indians, and to the number of about forty made their escape to Hutchinson, Minnesota. Similar events occurred at the Lower Agency on the same day, when nearly all the traders were butchered,

GEORGE SPENCER,
Who was Saved by Shaska, August, 1862.

and several who got away before the general massacre commenced were killed before reaching Fort Ridgely, thirteen miles below, or the other places of safety to which they were fleeing. All the buildings at both agencies were destroyed, but such property as was valuable to the Indians was carried off.

The news of the outbreak reached Fort Ridgely about 8 o'clock a. m. on the 18th of August through the arrival of a team from the Lower Agency, which brought a citizen badly wounded, but no details. Captain John F. Marsh, of the Fifth Minnesota, with eighty-five men, was holding the fort, and upon the news reaching him he transferred his command of the fort to Lieutenant Gere and with forty-five men started for the scene of hostilities. He had a full supply of ammunition, and with a six-mule team left the fort at 9 a. m. on the 18th of August, full of courage and anxious to get to the relief of the panic-stricken people. On the march up, evidences of the Indians' bloody work soon appeared, for bodies were found by the roadside of those who had recently been murdered, one of whom was Dr. Humphrey, surgeon at the agency. On reaching the vicinity of the ferry no Indians were in sight except one on the opposite side of the river, who endeavored to induce the soldiers to cross. A dense chapparal bordered the river on the agency side and tall grass covered the bottom land on the side where the troops were stationed. From various signs, suspicions were aroused of the presence of Indians, and the suspicions proved correct, for without a moment's notice, Indians in great numbers sprang up on all sides of the troops and opened a deadly fire. About half of the men were instantly killed. Finding themselves surrounded, desperate hand-to-hand encounters occurred, with varying results, and the remnant of the command made a point down the river about two miles from the ferry, Captain Marsh being among the number. They evidently attempted to cross, but Captain

Marsh was drowned in the effort, and only thirteen of his command escaped and reached the fort alive. Captain Marsh, in his excitement, may have erred in judgment and deemed it more his duty to attack than retreat; but the great odds of five hundred Indians to forty-five soldiers was too great and the captain and his brave men paid the penalty. He was young, brave and ambitious and knew but little of the Indians' tactics in war; but he no doubt believed he was doing his duty in advancing rather than retreating, and his countrymen will hold his memory and the memory of those who gave up their lives with him in warmer esteem than they would had he adopted the more prudent course of retracing his steps.

At a later date, in 1876, it will be remembered, the brave Custer was led into a similar trap, and of the five companies of the Seventh United States cavalry and their intrepid commanders only one was left to tell the tale.

After having massacred the people at the agencies, the Indians at once sent out marauding parties in all directions and covered the country from the northeast as far as Glencoe, Hutchinson and St. Peter, Minnesota, and as far south as Spirit Lake, Iowa. In their trail was to be found their deadly work of murder and devastation, for at least one thousand men, women and children were found brutally butchered, houses burned, and beautiful farms laid waste. The settlers, being accustomed to the friendly visits of these Indians, were taken completely unawares and were given no opportunity for defense.

Major Thomas Galbraith, the Sioux agent, had raised a company known as the Renville Rangers, and was expecting to report at Fort Snelling for muster and orders to proceed south to join one of the Minnesota commands;

but upon his arrival at St. Peter, on the evening of August 18, he learned the news of the outbreak at the agencies, and immediately retraced his steps, returning to Fort Ridgely, where he arrived on the 19th. On the same day Lieutenant Sheehan, of the Fifth Minnesota Infantry, with fifty men, arrived also, in obedience to a dispatch received from Captain Marsh, who commanded the post at Fort Ridgely. Lieutenant Sheehan, in enthusiasm and appearance, resembled General Sheridan. He was young and ambitious, and entered into this important work with such vim as to inspire his men to deeds of heroic valor. Upon receipt of Captain Marsh's dispatch ordering him to return at once, as "The Indians are raising hell at the Lower Agency!" he so inspired his men so as to make the forced march of forty-two miles in nine hours and a half, and he did not arrive a minute too soon. After Captain Marsh's death he became the ranking officer at Fort Ridgely, and the mantle of authority could not fall on more deserving shoulders. His command consisted of Companies B and C of the Fifth Minnesota, 100 men; Renville Rangers, 50 men; with several men of other organizations, including Sergeant John Jones (afterwards captain of artillery), and quite a number of citizen refugees, and a party that had been sent up by the Indian agent with the money to pay the Indians at the agency.

Designed by A. P. Connolly.

SIEGE OF FORT RIDGELY, AUGUST 20, 21 AND 22.

Indians fired the Fort with burning arrows, but were finally defeated by General Sibley's Column.

CHAPTER IX.

FORT RIDGLEY BESIEGED.

Fort Ridgely was a fort in name only. It was not built for defense, but was simply a collection of buildings built around a square facing inwards. The commandant's quarters, and those of the officers, also, were two-story structures of wood, while the men's barracks of two stories and the commissary storehouse were stone, and into these the families of the officers and soldiers and the refugee families were placed during the siege. On the 20th of August, 1862, about 3 p. m., an attack was made upon the fort by a large body of Indians, who stealthily came down the ravines and surrounded it. The first intimation the people and the garrison had of their proximity was a volley from the hostile muskets pouring between the openings of the buildings. The sudden onslaught caused great consternation, but order was soon restored.

Sergeant Jones, of the battery, who had seen service in the British army, as well as in our own regular army, in attempting to turn his guns on the Indians found to his utter astonishment that the pieces had been tampered with by some of the half-breeds belonging to the Renville Rangers who had deserted to the enemy. They had spiked the guns by ramming old rags into them. The sergeant soon made them serviceable, however, and brought his pieces to bear upon the Indians in such an effective way as to teach them a lesson in artillery practice they did not forget. The "rotten balls," as they termed the shells, fell thick and fast among them, and the havoc was so great that they withdrew out of range to hold a council of war and recover from their surprise. The fight lasted, however, for three hours, with a loss to the garrison of three killed and eighteen wounded. On the morning of Thursday, the 21st of August, the attack was renewed by the Indians, and they made a second attack in the afternoon, but with less force and earnestness and but little damage to the garrison. The soldiers were on the alert and the night was an anxious one, for the signs from the hostiles indicated that they were making preparations for a further attempt to capture the fort. During the night barricades were placed at all open spaces between the buildings, and the little garrison band instructed, each man's duty specified, and directions given to the women and children, who were placed in the stone barracks, to lie low so as not to be harmed by bullets coming in at the windows. On Friday, the 22d, Little Crow, the then Sioux commander in chief, had the fort surrounded by 650 warriors whom he had brought down from the agency. He had them concealed in the ravines which surrounded the fort, and endeavored by sending a few of the warriors out on the open prairie to draw the garrison out from the fort, but fortunately there were men there who had previously had experience in Indian warfare, and the scheme of this wily old Indian fox did not work. Little Crow, finding it useless to further maneuver in this way, ordered an attack. The showers of bullets continued for seven long hours, or until about 7 p. m., but the attack was courageously and bitterly opposed by the infantry, and this, together with the skillfully handled artillery by Sergeant Jones, saved the garrison for another day. The Indians sought shelter behind and in the outlying wooden buildings, but well directed shells from the battery fired these buildings and routed the Indians, who in turn made various attempts by means of fire arrows to ignite the wooden buildings of the fort proper. But for the daring and vigilance of the troops the enemy would have succeeded in their purpose. The Indians lost heavily in this engagement, while the loss to the troops was one killed and seven wounded. Lieutenant Sheehan, the commander of the post, was a man of true grit, and he was ably assisted by Lieutenant Gorman of the Renville Rangers, and Sergeants Jones and McGrau of the battery. Every man was a hero and did his whole duty. Surrounded as they were by hundreds of bloodthirsty savages, this little band was all that stood between the hundreds of women and children refugees and certain death, or worse than death! Besides, the government storehouses were filled with army supplies, and about $75,000 in gold, with which they intended making an annuity payment to these same Indians.

The water supply being cut off, the soldiers and all the people, especially the wounded, suffered severely, but Post Surgeon Mueller and his noble wife heroically responded to the urgent calls of the wounded sufferers irrespective of danger. Mrs. Mueller was a lovely woman of the heroic type. During the siege, in addition to caring for the wounded, she made coffee, and in the night frequently visited all the men who were on guard and plentifully supplied them with this exhilarating beverage. An incident in relation to her also is, that during the siege the Indians had sheltered themselves behind a hay stack and from it were doing deadly work. Sergeant Jones could not bring his twenty-four pounder to bear on them without exposing his men too much, unless he fired directly through a building that stood in the way. This house was built as they are on the plantations in the South, with a broad hall running from the front porch clear through to the rear. In the rear of this hall were rough double doors, closed principally in winter time to keep the snow from driving through. The sergeant had them closed and then brought his piece around in front, and the Indians away back of the house could not see what the maneuvering was. He crept up and attached a rope to the handle of the door, and looking through the cracks got the range and then sighted his gun. Mrs. Mueller, sheltered and out of harm's way, held the end of the attached rope. The signal for her to pull open the doors was given by Sergeant Jones, and this signal was the dropping of a handkerchief. When the signal came, with good nerve, she pulled the rope and open flew the doors. Immediately the gunner pulled the lanyard and the shell with lighted fuse landed in the haystacks, which were at once set fire to and the Indians dislodged. This lady died at her post, beloved by all who knew her, and a grateful government has erected an expensive monument over her remains, which lie buried in the soldiers' cemetery at Fort Ridgely, where, with hundreds of others whose pathway to the grave was smoothed by her motherly hands, they will remain until the great reveille on the resurrection dawn.

LITTLE CROW.

CHAPTER X.

SIEGE OF NEW ULM.

Little Crow, finding himself baffled in his attempt to capture the fort, and learning from his scouts that Colonel Sibley was on his way with two regiments to relieve the garrison, concentrated all his forces and proceeded to New

Ulm, about thirteen miles distant, which he intended to wipe out the next morning. Here, again, he was disappointed. The hero of New Ulm was Hon. Charles E. Flandreau, who deserves more than a passing notice. By profession he is a lawyer, and at this time was a judge on the bench, and is now enjoying a lucrative practice in St. Paul. By nature he is an organizer and a leader, and to his intrepid bravery and wise judgment New Ulm and her inhabitants owe their salvation from the savagery of Little Crow and his bloodthirsty followers. He had received the news of the outbreak at his home near St. Peter in the early morning of August 19, and at once decided what should be done to save the people.

His duty to wife and children was apparent, and to place them in safety was his first thought, which he did by taking them to St. Peter. He then issued a call for volunteers, and in response to this soon found himself surrounded by men who needed no second bidding, for the very air was freighted with the terror of the situation. Armed with guns of any and all descriptions, with bottles of powder, boxes of caps and pockets filled with bullets, one hundred and twenty men, determined on revenge, pressed forward to meet this terrible foe.

Where should they go? Rumors came from all directions, and one was that Fort Ridgely was being besieged and had probably already fallen. Their eyes also turned toward New Ulm, which was but thirteen miles distant and in an absolutely unprotected condition. Its affrighted people were at the mercy of this relentless enemy. The work Judge Flandreau performed in perfecting an organization was masterful, for the men who flocked in and offered their services he could not control in a military sense, because they were not enlisted. The emergency was very great and it was necessary to do the right thing and at the right time and to strike hard and deadly blows, and trusted men were sent forward to scout and report. Hon. Henry A. Swift, afterwards governor of Minnesota, rendered good service in company with William G. Hayden as they scouted the country in a buggy. It was a novel way to scout, but horses were too scarce to allow a horse to each. An advance guard was sent forward about noon, and an hour later the balance of the command was in motion, eagerly pushing forward and anxious to meet the enemy wherever he might be found. The advance guard which Flandreau sent out to determine whether Fort Ridgely or New Ulm should be the objective point had not yet been heard from, and, that no time might be lost, he determined that he would push forward to New Ulm, and if that village was safe he would turn his attention to Ridgely. He found his guard at New Ulm, and they had been largely reinforced by other men who came in to help protect the place. They arrived just in time to assist in repelling an attack of about two hundred Indians, who had suddenly surrounded the little village. Before the arrival of Flandreau and his command they could see the burning houses in the distance, and by this they knew that the work of devastation had commenced, and the forced march was kept up. The rain was pouring in torrents, and yet they had made thirty-two miles in seven hours and reached the place about 8 o'clock in the evening.

The next day reinforcements continued to come in from various points until the little army of occupation numbered three hundred effective and determined men. A council of war was called and a line of defense determined upon by throwing up barricades in nearly all the streets.

The situation was a very grave one and it was soon apparent that a one-man power was necessary—that a guiding mind must control the actions of this hastily gathered army of raw material; and to this end, Judge Flandreau was declared generalissimo, and subsequent events proved that the selection was a most judicious one. In a few days subsequent to this he received a commission as colonel from Governor Ramsey and was placed in command of all irregular troops. There were fifty companies reported to him all told; some were mounted and others were not. His district extended from New Ulm, Minnesota, to Sioux City, Iowa. It was a most important command, and Colonel Flandreau proved himself a hero as well as a competent organizer. He is so modest about it even to-day that he rarely refers to it.

A provost guard was at once established, order inaugurated, defenses strengthened and confidence partially restored. Nothing serious transpired until Saturday morning at about 9 o'clock, when 650 Indians, who had been so handsomely repulsed at Fort Ridgely, thirteen miles above, made a determined assault upon the town, driving in the pickets. The lines faltered for a time, but soon rallied and steadily held the enemy at bay. The Indians had surrounded the town and commenced firing the buildings, and the conflagration was soon raging on both sides of the main street in the lower part of the town, and the total destruction of the place seemed inevitable. It was necessary to dislodge the enemy in some way, so a squad of fifty men was ordered out to charge down the burning street, and the Indians were driven out. The soldiers then burned everything and the battle was won. The desperate character of the fighting may be judged when we find the casualties to be ten men killed and fifty wounded in about an hour and a half, and this out of a much depleted force, for out of the little army of three hundred men, seventy-five who had been sent under Lieutenant Huey to guard the ferry were cut off and forced to retreat towards St. Peter. Before reaching this place, however, they met reinforcements and returned to the attack. The Indians now, in turn, seeing quite a reinforcement coming, thought it wise to retreat, and drew off to the northward, in the direction of the fort, and disappeared.

The little town of New Ulm at this time contained from 1,200 to 1,500 non-combatants, consisting of women and children, refugees and unarmed citizens, every individual of whom would have been massacred if it had not been for this brave band of men under the command of Colonel Flandreau. Not knowing what the retreat of the Indians indicated, the uncertainty and scarcity of provisions, the pestilence to be feared from stench and exposure, all combined to bring about the decision to evacuate the town and try to reach Mankato. In order to do this a train was made up, into which were loaded the women and children and about eighty wounded men. It was a sad sight to witness this enforced breaking up of home ties, homes burned and farms and gardens laid waste, loved ones dead and wounded, and this one of the inevitable results of an unnecessary and unprovoked war. The march to Mankato was without special incident. Especially fortunate was this little train of escaping people in not meeting any wandering party of hostile Indians.

The first day about half the distance from Mankato to St. Peter was covered; the main column was pushed on to its final destination, it being the intention of Colonel Flandreau to return with a portion of his command to New Ulm, or remain where they were, so as to keep a force between the Indians and the settlements. But the men of his command, not having heard a word from their families for over a week, felt apprehensive and refused to return or remain, holding that the protection of their families was paramount to all other considerations. It must be remembered that these men were not soldiers, but had demonstrated their willingness to fight when necessary, and they did fight, and left many of their comrades dead and wounded on the battlefield. The train that had been sent forward arrived in Mankato on the 25th of August, and the balance of the command reached the town on the day following, when the men sought their homes.

The stubborn resistance the Indians met with at Fort Ridgely and New Ulm caused them to withdraw to their own country, and this temporary lull in hostilities enabled the whites to more thoroughly organize, and the troops to prepare for a campaign up into the Yellow Medicine country, where it was known a large number of captives were held.

COLONEL CHARLES E. FLANDREAU,

Who was in command at New Ulm, Minn., during the Siege from
August 20th to 25th, 1862.

CHAPTER XI.

COL. FLANDREAU IN COMMAND.

While the exciting events narrated in the previous chapters were taking place other portions of the state were preparing for defense. At Forest City, Hutchinson, Glencoe, and even as far south as St. Paul and Minneapolis, men were rapidly organizing for home protection. In addition to the Sioux, the Chippewas and Winnebagoes were becoming affected and seemed anxious for a pretext to don the paint and take the warpath. Colonel Flandreau having received his commission as colonel from Governor Ramsey, with authority to take command of the Blue Earth country extending from New Ulm to the Iowa line, embracing the western and southwestern frontier of the state, proceeded at once to properly organize troops, commission officers, and do everything in his power as a military officer to give protection to the citizens. The Colonel established his headquarters at South Bend and the home guards came pouring in, reporting for duty, and squads that had been raised and mustered into the volunteer service, but had not yet joined their commands, were organized into companies, and the Colonel soon found himself surrounded by quite an army of good men, well officered, and with a determination to do their whole duty. This was done by establishing a cordon of military posts so as to inspire confidence and prevent an exodus of the people. Any one who has not been through the ordeal of an Indian insurrection can form no idea of the terrible apprehension that takes possession of a defenseless and non-combatant people under such circumstances.

The mystery and suspense attending an Indian's movements, and the certainty of the cruelty to his captives, strikes terror to the heart, and upon the first crack of his rifle a thousand are put to flight. While cruelty is one of the natural characteristics of the Indians, yet there are many among them who have humane feelings and are susceptible of Christian influences. As friends, they are of the truest; but the thoughtless cry out as did the enemies of our Savior: "Crucify him! Crucify him!" Other Day, Standing Buffalo, Shaska and Old Betz were as true and as good people as ever lived, and yet they are held responsible for the atrocities of their savage brethren. At the risk of their own lives they warned hundreds of people and guided them by night, and hid them by day, until finally they reached a place of safety. At the hostile camp, where they had over four hundred women and children, it was only through the influence of these and other sturdy friendly chiefs that any lives were saved. They had to even throw barricades around their tepees and watch day and night until the soldiers came, giving notice that whoever raised hand to harm these defenseless people would do it at their peril. When we know of these kind acts, let us pause a moment before we say there are no good Indians.

It was a study to look at some of these old dusky heroes, who said nothing but thought much, and who had determined that, come what would, harm should not come to the captives. There were statesmen, too, among them;

men wise in council, who had respect for their Great Father at Washington, who were cognizant of the fact that much dissatisfaction was engendered among their people by occurrences taking place at the time of the negotiation for the treaties. They counselled their people, and no doubt tried hard to induce them to forsake their desire for vengeance on the whites, and thus retard the progress they were making for their offspring toward civilization and a better manner of living.

You might properly ask here: "What became of the friendly Indians while the hostiles were on the war-path?" Some of them forgot their friendly feelings and, like the whisky victim, when they got a taste of blood, they wanted more! They were all forced by the hostiles to don their war paint and breech-cloth, and go with them against the whites, and they were wise enough to know that it was folly to resist. Their main object was to prevent the wholesale murder of the captives, for when hostitlties opened, they knew if they did not go, every woman and child in the captive camp would be murdered; and the friendlies would be blamed as much as the hostiles themselves.

MRS. ESTLICK AND CHILDREN.

CHAPTER XII.

MRS. EASTLICK AND FAMILY.

The note of alarm sounded throughout the neighborhood and without a moment's warning hurried preparations were made for the exodus. Women and children and a few household goods were loaded into wagons and a start made for a place of safety. Indians suddenly appeared and commenced an indiscriminate fire upon the terror-stricken refugees.

The individual cases of woman's heroism, daring, bravery, cunning and strong-willed self-sacrifice, could be recounted by the score, and in some instances are past belief. Their achievements would be considered as pure fiction but for our own personal knowledge. Many of the real occurrences would seem like legends, when the father had been murdered and the mother left with two, three and even five and six children to care for, and if possible save them from the ferocity of the painted red devils, whose thirst for blood could seemingly not be satiated. One noted case was the Eastlick family, and this was only one of a hundred. Eleven men of the party had already been killed, and Mr. Eastlick among the number. The women with their children were scattered in all directions in the brush, to escape if possible the inevitable fate in store for them if caught. The Indians shouted to them to come out from their hiding places and surrender and they should be spared. The remaining men, thinking perhaps their lives might be saved if they surrendered, urged their wives to do so, and the men would, if possible, escape and give the alarm. Thus, without a word or a look lest they should betray the remaining husbands, were these women driven from their natural protectors and obliged to submit to the tender mercies of their hated red captors. The supposed dead husbands watched the receding forms of their devoted wives, whom in all likelihood they never would see again. Burton Eastlick, the fifteen-year-old boy, could not endure the thought of leaving his mother to this uncertain fate, and he followed her, but she persuaded him, for the sake of his fifteen-months-old baby brother, to leave her and try and make his escape, carrying the little one with him. And how well did he execute his mission.

The Indians fired upon the little group and Mrs. Eastlick fell, wounded in three places, and the boy ran away, supposing his mother dead; but she revived, and crawled to where her wounded husband and six-year-old boy were, to find both dead. Can you picture such a scene or imagine what the feelings of this poor mother must be under these awful circumstances? Sublime silence reigning over earth and sky, and she alone with her dead!

What a parting must that have been from husband and child—death and desolation complete. Could she look to her God? A heart of faith so sorely tried, and yet she said: "I am in His hands; surely I must trust Him, for I am yet alive, and two precious children, Burton and little baby, are fleeing to a place of safety."

This heroic boy, Burton, seeing his mother shot, and supposed to be dead, and watching the life flicker and the spirit of his six-year-old brother pass away, placed the dear little body beside that of his father, and with a bravery born of an heroic nature he accepted his charge, and with the injunction of his precious, dying mother still ringing in his ears, made preparations to start. It seemed an herculean effort, but the brave boy said: "We may yet be saved!" So, pressing his baby brother close to his heart, he took a last look upon the faces of his dear father, mother and six-year-old brother and started.

Ninety miles, thick with dangers, lay before our young hero; but he faltered not. When tired carrying his little brother in his arms he took him on his back. The first day he made sixteen miles, and in ten consecutive days covered sixty miles. He lived on corn and such food as he could find in deserted houses. At night his bed was the earth, his pillow a stone, and the sky his only covering, the bright stars acting as nightly sentinels over him, as weary, he and his little baby charge slept. If angels have a duty to perform, surely troops of them must have hovered around. He fed the little brother as best he could to appease his hunger and covered him as with angel wings to protect the little trembling body from the chilly night air. Brave boy! The pages of history furnish nothing more noble than this deed, and if you yet live, what a consolation, what a proud reflection, to know that there never before was witnessed a deed more deserving of immortal fame.

"Thou shalt not be afraid for the terror by night, nor for the arrow that flyeth by day." The resolute mother, badly wounded and left for dead, revived. She looked upon the face of her dead husband and little boy, and with sublime courage started for a place of safety. At the risk of being discovered and murdered—hungry, tired, with wounds undressed and a heavy, aching heart and deathly sick, she was obliged to lie by for some time, after which she again started, and for ten days and nights this poor sorrow-stricken woman traveled on her weary way.

Providence led her in the path of a mail carrier on a route from Sioux Falls City, in Dakota, to New Ulm, Minnesota. He had formerly known her, but in her emaciated, jaded, pitiful condition the change was so great he did not recognize her.

At New Ulm she found her children, where they were

being kindly cared for, having been found in the tall grass nearly dead from exposure and starvation. Thus the remaining portion of the family were reunited on earth, and it is proper to here draw the curtain and allow them a few moments for communion, that the fountain of the heart which had been dried up by the awful occurrences of the previous few days might unbidden flow. The mother's heart was nearly crushed with the thought of husband and child—victims of the ferocious Indians, killed and yet unburied on the prairie nearly one hundred miles away; but, mother-like, she rejoiced in finding the two children who had wandered so far and through a kind Providence escaped so many dangers.

ESCAPE OF THE MISSIONARIES.

CHAPTER XIII.

THE MISSIONARIES—THEIR ESCAPE.

A few miles above the Yellow Medicine were the churches and schools of the Rev. S. R. Riggs and Dr. Williamson. Both of these gentlemen had long been missionaries among the Indians and had gained their confidence; and in return had placed the most implicit confidence in them. But these good men had been warned to flee for their lives, and they reluctantly gathered together a few household treasures, and placing themselves and families under the guidance of Providence, started for a place of safety. Fort Ridgely was their objective point, but they learned that the place was being besieged and that it would be unsafe to proceed further in this direction, so turned their weary steps toward Henderson, Minnesota.

With courage braced up, weary in body and anxious in mind, they went into camp until the morning. "The pillar of cloud by day, and the pillar of fire by night," guided this anxious band through a most trying and perilous journey, but they gained the settlement at last and were among friends. In leaving their little homes, where they had found so much pleasure in the work of the Master, in pointing the Indians to a better way of living, they were sorrowful; but, like Abraham of old, faithful in their allegiance to God, not daring to question His ways in compelling them to turn their backs upon their chosen work—

His work. The missionaries and teachers formed strong attachments among this dusky race. In their communion with them they found them ready and eager to converse about the Great Spirit and to learn of the wonderful things taught in the Bible. They loved to sing, and the melody of sacred song found a responsive chord in their souls as they were gradually emerging from their barbarous condition, and coming into the full light of a Christian salvation. In conversation with the writer, Mr. Riggs once said that as he was passing one of their happy little homes he could hear the squaw mother, in her peculiar plaintive tones, singing to her little children:

> "Jesus Christ, nitowashte kin
> Woptecashni mayaqu"—
> Jesus Christ, Thy Loving Kindness,
> Boundlessly, Thou Givest Me.

She had become a Christian mother through the teachings of the missionaries. Her maternal affection was as deep and abiding as in the breast of her more favored white sister, and her eye of faith looked beyond the stars to the happy hunting ground, where the Greater Spirit abides, and with the assurance that some day she and all her race would stand with the redeemed in the presence of the Judge of all the worlds. The Christian missionary felt for these people as no one else could; and, while not trying nor desiring to excuse them for their unholy war against the whites, yet they could not persuade themselves to believe that they had been justly dealt with by civilized America.

LITTLE PAUL.

CHAPTER XIV.

THE INDIAN POW-WOW.

The Indians of the various tribes of the Upper and Lower Sioux—the Sissitons, the Tetons, the Yanktons and the Yanktonnais and other tribes held a pow-wow to try and force a conclusion of the war, and some of their ablest men, their statesmen, were present, and their views you have here verbatim. More decorum prevailed among them, and they were more deliberate than is observed in the average white man's convention. Little Crow had his supporters present, and a very fluent Yanktonnais Sioux traced on the ground a map of the country, showing the course of the Missouri River and the locality of the different forts. He marked out the mountains, seas and oceans, and stated that an army, great in numbers, was coming from across the country to assist them. This gave rise to the unfounded rumor referred to in another chapter, that emissaries from the South were among them to incite them to war.

John Paul, or Little Paul, was friendly to the whites, and in a speech to the Indians at this pow-wow said:

"I am friendly to the whites, and will deliver these women and children at Fort Ridgely. I am opposed to the war on the whites. You say you are brave men, and can whip the whites. That is a lie—persons who cut women and children's throats are not brave. You are squaws and cowards. Fight the whites if you want to, but do it like brave men. I am ashamed of the way you have acted towards the captives; and, if any of you have the feelings of men, you will give them up. You may look fierce at me, but I am not afraid of you."

Red Iron, one of the chiefs of the Upper Indians, was not friendly. He was one of the principal chiefs of the Sissitons, and at one time was so outspoken against the whites that Governor Ramsey, who was then Superintendent of Indian Affairs, and was at the agency, had occasion to rebuke him in a substantial way—he reduced him to the ranks. In other words, he broke him of his chieftianship. This was in December, 1852.

Red Iron was a handsome Indian, an athlete, six feet in his moccasins, with a large, well-developed head, aquiline nose, thin lips, but with intelligence and resolution beaming all over his countenance.

When brought into the presence of Governor Ramsey he walked with a firm, lordly tread, and was clad in half military and half Indian costume. When he came in he seated

RED IRON.

himself in silence, which was not broken until through an interpreter the Governor asked him what excuse he had to offer for not coming to the council when sent for.

Red Iron, when he arose to his feet to reply, did so with

a Chesterfieldian grace, allowing his blanket to fall from his shoulders, and, intentionally dropping his pipe of peace. He stood before the Governor for a moment in silence, with his arms folded, his bearing betraying perfect self-composure, a defiant smile playing upon his lips. In a firm voice he said:

Red Iron—"I started to come, but your braves drove me back."

Governor—"What excuse have you for not coming the second time I sent for you?"

Red Iron—"No other excuse than I have already given you."

When the Governor, as Commissioner of Indian Affairs, informed this proud chief that, by virtue of his office, he would break him of his chieftianship it appealed to his pride, and he said:

"You break me? I was elected chief by my tribe. You can't break me."

The chief, while surrendering to the powers that be, never felt friendly to the whites, and during this war of which we write he continued stubborn and sullen to the end.

Standing Buffalo, hereditary chief of the Sissitons, was a different type, and counselled living in peace, but desired fair treatment and honest dealings with his people. He was a handsome Indian, and a man of rare ability. General Sibley was anxious to know how he felt on the important question agitating the Sioux Nation, and desired his cooperation in liberating the captives and compassing the capture of Little Crow and his followers. At this Indian convention this noted chief said:

"I am a young man, but I have always felt friendly

toward the whites, because they were kind to my father. You have brought me into great danger without my knowledge of it beforehand. By killing the whites, it is just as if you had waited for me in ambush and shot me down.

STANDING BUFFALO.

You Lower Indians feel bad because we have all got into this trouble; but I feel worse, because I know that neither I nor my people have killed any of the whites, and that yet we have to suffer with the guilty. I was out buffalo hunting when I heard of the outbreak, and I felt as if I was dead, and I feel so now. You all know that the Indians cannot live without the aid of the white man, and, therefore, I have made up my mind that Paul is right, and my Indians will stand by him. We claim this reservation. What are you doing here? If you want to fight the whites, go back and fight them. Leave my village at Big Stone Lake. You sent word to my young men to come down, and that you had plenty of oxen, horses, goods, powder and lead, and now we see nothing. We are going back to Big Stone Lake and leave you to fight the whites. Those who make peace can say that Standing Buffalo and his people will give themselves up in the spring."

They kept their word, and would have nothing to do with Little Crow.

Standing Buffalo was killed in 1863 by an accident.

Other Day, a civilized Indian, in addressing the council at this time, said:

"You can, of course, easily kill a few unarmed whites, but it would be a cowardly thing to do, because we have gained their confidence, and the innocent will suffer with the guilty, and the great Father at Washington will send his soldiers to punish you, and we will all suffer. I will not join you in this, but will help defend these white people who have always been our friends."

Other Day was a true friend of the whites; he looked it. He was a full-blood Indian, it is true, and the Indians respected and feared him, but his desire to forsake the barbarous teachings of his father inclined him towards the unsuspecting settlers.

In 1863 he was General Sibley's most trusted and confidential scout. In the early outbreak Other Day manifested his loyalty to his white friends by risking his life in their defense, piloting sixty people through the river bottoms during the nights to a place of safety. He traveled with his charge in the night, and hid them in underbrush during the daytime. He was a true-hearted, kind man, with a red skin, who has gone to his reward in a land where there are no reds, no blacks, but where all are white.

Little Crow, who is one of the principal characters in this narrative, was an Indian of no mean ability. He was the commander-in-chief of the hostile tribes, and wielded a powerful influence among all the tribes of this great Sioux Nation. He was a powerful man, and felt his lordly position; was confident of final success, and very defiant at the outset. He had a penchant for notoriety in more ways than one. In dress he was peculiar, and could nearly always be found with some parts of a white man's clothing. He was particularly conspicuous in the style of collar he wore; happy in the possession of one of the old-style standing collars, such as Daniel Webster and other old-time gentlemen bedecked themselves with. He also possessed a black silk neckerchief and a black frock coat, and on grand occasions wore both.

He had strongly marked features, and in studying the lineaments of his face one would not adjudge him a particularly bad Indian. As we had hundreds of these men in our custody, a good opportunity was offered while guarding them to try one's gift as a reader of character as stamped in the face, but Little Crow proved an enigma. It was like a novice trying to separate good money from bad, an unprofitable and unsuccessful task. Little Crow said:

"It is impossible to make peace if we so desired. Did we ever do the most trifling thing, the whites would hang us.

Now, we have been killing them by the hundreds in Dakota, Minnesota and Iowa, and I know if they get us into their hands they will hang every one of us. As for me, I will kill as many of them as I can, and fight them till I die. Do not think you will escape. There is not a band of Indians from the Redwood Agency to Big Stone Lake that has not had some of its members embroiled in this war. I tell you we must fight and perish together. A man is a fool and coward who thinks otherwise, and who will desert his nation at such a time. Disgrace not yourselves by a surrender to those who will hang you up like dogs; but die, if die you must, with arms in your hands, like warriors and braves of the Dakotas."

In one of our battles we took some fine-looking bucks prisoners, and the soldiers were for scalping them at once, but we had a little "pow-wow" with them, and found them intelligent and well educated; they were students home on a vacation from Bishop Whipple's school at Faribault, Minnesota, and said they were forced, much against their will, to go on the warpath; that they had not fired a bullet at the whites; that they fired blank cartridges because they felt friendly to the whites, and had no desire to kill them. There were three of them; we told them they could take their choice—be shot or enlist; they chose the latter, and went South with us, staying until the close of the Rebellion, and they displayed the courage of the born soldier

BREVET MAJOR GENERAL H. H. SIBLEY,
Commander in the field in 1862 and 1863 against the Sioux Indians.

CHAPTER XV.

GOV. SIBLEY APPOINTED COMMANDER.

While these scenes which I have related were being enacted in the upper country excitement ran high at St. Paul, and for a time the great struggle then going on in the South was forgotten. The news of the outbreak soon reached St. Paul, and couriers, with horses covered with foam, kept coming in one after another, until the officers at Fort Snelling were ordered by Governor Ramsey to be in readiness with their men to move at a moment's notice, and we did not have long to wait.

The Sixth Minnesota, of which I was a member, had just organized, and was assigned to Hancock corps, Army of the Potomac, but the events transpiring in the Indian country made it necessary for all available troops to go there. When I say that the whole country was seething with excitement it is no exaggeration. The towns, big and little, were filled with frightened refugees; the rumors that came in were of the most frightful nature, and the whole state was clamorous for protection.

Governor Ramsey, in his desire to protect the panic-stricken people and liberate the captives, cast about for a suitable commander for this important work. Of all the men in and about St. Paul who seemed eminently qualified for this position, Governor Henry H. Sibley, who at that time was living in quietude in his home in Mendota, just across the river from the fort, was his choice.

Governor Henry Hastings Sibley, the hero of these Indian campaigns, was born in the city of Detroit February 20, 1811. His sire was Chief Justice Solomon Sibley, of Detroit, and his mother was Sarah Whipple Sproat, whose father, Colonel Ebenezer Sproat, was an accomplished officer of the Continental army, and the granddaughter of Commodore Abraham Whipple, an illustrious commander in the Continental navy. He came from a long line of illustrious ancestry on both sides, of good Puritan stock, and dating his lineage back to the Sibleys of William the Conqueror of England in the fifteenth century.

He was not a fighter; his heart was too tender for that, but he felt the weighty responsibility he had assumed when he consented to lead the soldiers and save the lives of the captives. For delaying he was denounced on all hands. The press denounced him for not falling immediately upon the Indians; but he knew the enemy better than his censors. If he had heeded the behests of the clamorous people not a captive would have been spared; but to-day hundreds live to bless him for his cautious, conservative movements. Until his death, which occurred but a few months since, he lived in his beautiful home in St. Paul; and, although a half century of winters in the far Northwest had whitened his head, and a great deal more than a half century of time had made his limbs tremble, neither time nor frost had sapped the citadel of his mind. He was a member of Aker Post, No. 21, Department of Minnesota, and the comrades, in deference to his declining years, went in a body to his beautiful home where he was mustered in. He lived in peace and plenty, surrounded by his family and friends, who esteemed him for his worth. He passed away respected and regretted by a host of friends throughout the land, who knew him as a citizen and a soldier. I knew him personally and intimately since 1857; and in his death, with others great in our nation's history, we are reminded that in war the bullet is no respecter of rank; the commander and the soldier fall together.

Governor Sibley was commissioned by Governor Ramsey as Colonel of Volunteers, and assigned to the command of the expedition. He was selected because he had spent many years of his life among the Indians as a trader, he spoke their language, he knew them personally, and knew their characteristics. He was a man of large experience, education and ability, and possessed, withal, a cool head. He knew the Indians, and they knew him and respected him. He consented to lead the forces against the Indians when appealed to by Governor Ramsey, upon conditions that he should not be interfered with by His Excellency, or any one else, and that he should have adequate supplies of men, stores and transportation. Colonel Sibley, afterwards Brigadier and Brevet Major-General of Volunteers, with his staff and Companies A, B, and E, of the Sixth Minnesota Infantry, embarked on a small steamer then at anchor near the fort, and steamed up the Minnesota river to Shakopee, distant about forty miles by water. We started in a furious rain, and after a slow trip up the narrow and winding Minnesota, arrived at Shakopee, where we found the frightened citizens ready to receive us with open arms, although all the firearms we had were worthless and condemned Austrian rifles, without ammunition to fit them. All serviceable material of war had been shipped to the South. Our first guard duty was on picket in the suburbs of Shakopee, and our instructions were to press all teams into the service. We felt the gravity of the situation, and obeyed orders to the letter as nearly as we, raw recruits, could. While here the news was spread that Indians were in the vicinity, and the women and children began to flock to the vicinity of the soldiers; the alarm was without foundation. As we were stationed on the various roads leading to and from the town, the citizens who had been so badly scared seemed to feel comparatively safe. The news from the upper country, however, was discouraging, and appeals for protection very urgent. We could not move at once from lack of transportation, and had no adequate supplies, either of food, arms or ammunition, for we had been so hurriedly dispatched from Fort Snelling that only about half of one company had been supplied with even the worthless muskets spoken of, and the whole command with but two days' rations. It was necessary, however, to make some quick demonstration to appease the panic-stricken people. After a delay of one day, by various routes by land and water, the regiment concentrated at St. Peter, under command of Colonel William Crooks, where it was inspected and remained four or five days, awaiting the receipt of suitable arms and ammunition and also reinforcements.

Our guns were so absolutely worthless that it was necessary to delay a little, as the Indians, in large numbers, were then besieging Fort Ridgely, and were well armed with Springfield rifles, while our own arms were condemned Austrian muskets.

We embarked on a boat at Shakopee and sailed up to Carver, forty miles above, and there pressed in teams to carry us through what was known as the "Big Woods."

It had been raining for days, and the town of Carver was literally packed with refugees. There was not an empty building in it, even the warehouses were filled, and the muddy streets were a sight to behold. The mud was ankle deep, and you may imagine in what condition everything was. I cannot describe it.

The frightened people, who had flocked in from all the country round, told most woeful tales of Indian atrocities. In some cases they were overdrawn, but later on we saw evidences enough to warrant them fleeing to a place of safety. There was no safety, however, in coming to these small towns, for they were without protection.

After loading up the teams, we started through the "Big Woods," and the roads were in such a horrible condition that we made but slow progress. However, we had to make Glencoe, twenty-five miles distant, before night or camp down in the woods in the mud. It became pitchy dark, but we kept on the move, and in time got through the woods and could see the lights of Glencoe afar off. This was only a small place, but the twinkling lights from the houses were a pleasant sight, and when we arrived there the people were glad to see us. We remained over night, and the next day started for St. Peter. We could see evidences of Indian devastation in every direction, among which were the burning buildings and grain stacks on the beautiful neighboring farms.

On the route to St. Peter, which we reached early in the evening, we discovered a few dead settlers, and took some families along with us. Upon our arrival we went into camp with the rest of the command, and were soon placed under strict military discipline, and in a brief time our commander, Colonel William Crooks, a West Pointer, brought order out of chaos.

Of the preparation and forward march to relieve Fort Ridgely I will reserve for another chapter.

CHAPTER XVI.

MARCH TO FORT RIDGELY.

In the interval the companies were drilled and the command otherwise prepared to act effectively against the formidable body of hostile warriors, who were well armed and plentifully supplied with powder and ball. Colonel Sibley, having looked the ground over with a critical eye, uninfluenced by the public clamor and fault-finding of the press, remained firm in the determination not to take the field until assured of success in his operations. He knew the Indians well, and knew it was necessary to fight or failure, there would be no adequate barrier to the descent of the savages upon St. Paul and Minneapolis, and the desolation of the state generally. The Chippewas on the north were known to be in secret communication with Little Crow, the head of the Sioux hordes, and ready to them cautiously if he would succeed, for, in case of defeat co-operate with him if victorious, while the Winnebagos were also in active sympathy with him, for two or three of their warriors were found among the dead after the battle of Wood Lake, which occurred later on. Arms, ammunition and supplies arriving, we took up the line of march for Fort Ridgely, which was then in a state of seige. Our advent at the Fort was hailed with delight, for the little garrison was pretty well tired out with the fighting and watching that they had had on their hands for the eight days previous. Barricades had been erected at all weak points, but the Indians so far outnumbered the soldiers that they approached near enough to fire the wooden buildings of the fort proper in many places.

Our march to Fort Ridgely was the first we had made as an entire organization, and under an able commanding officer we profited by it. On the way we found the dead body of a colored man from St. Paul by the name of Taylor. He was a barber by trade, but also quite a noted gambler, and had been up to the agency to get his share of the money when the Indians got their pay.

He played one game too many, and lost—his life.

Before we reached the Fort the Indians took alarm and sullenly retreated upon our approach, after having done all possible damage to men and property. As we entered, the brave little garrison accompanied by the women and children turned out to greet us, and a right joyous time we had. A detachment of thirty men of the Fifth Minnesota, under Captain Marsh, the commander of the fort, upon receipt of news of the outbreak, had marched in the direction of the Lower Sioux Agency, distant a few miles. The Indians, perceiving the advance of this small detachment, placed themselves in ambush in the long grass at the crossing of the Minnesota River and awaited the oncoming of their unsuspecting victims, and, when in the toils, they opened a terrific fire upon them, which destroyed almost the entire party.

Colonel Sibley hurried forward supplies and ammunition for an extensive campaign, for, from his knowledge of the Indians, he knew it was no boy's play. The moving spirit among the hostiles was Little Crow, a wily old chief, without principle, but active and influential. He had harangued his people into the belief that the fight going on among the whites in the South had drawn off all the able-bodied men, leaving none but old men, women and children. "Now," he said, "is the time to strike for Minnesota. These fertile fields, stolen from us, are ours; the buffalo are gone; we have no food, and our women and children are starving. Let the warriors assemble in war paint and drive the pale-faces from the face of the earth!" He told his people they could pitch their wigwams the coming winter in St. Paul and hold high carnival in the legislative halls. So widespread had the alarm became that it reached St. Paul and Minneapolis, and "minute men" were on duty on the bluffs adjacent for several days. In addition to the Sioux, the Chippewas and Winnebagos were becoming very restless, and this caused additional uneasiness in the two cities.

Colonel Sibley, upon his arrival of the fort, sent out scouts to ascertain the whereabouts of the Indians. The news they brought was that a large camp of hostiles was located above the Yellow Medicine, where they held as captives about four hundred white women and children, and one white man. They also reported that the Indians were preparing to make a raid on the small towns below the fort.

It was also known that a large number of citizens who had been killed near the agency were yet unburied, and the fate of Captain Marsh and his men was in doubt. To this end a small command was organized, as narrated in another chapter, to go out to bury the dead and relieve Captain Marsh and his men if they were found alive.

CHAPTER XVII.

BURIAL OF CAPT. MARSH AND MEN.

Company "A," of the Sixth Minnesota, together with two men each from the other companies, were detailed to accompany a burial party, with instructions to properly bury all bodies found, and, if possible, ascertain the fate of Captain Marsh and his thirty men, who had gone out to intercept the Indians at the Redwood Crossing. In addition to this detail we had a small detachment of citizen cavalry, under Captain Joe Anderson, to act as scouts.

Our little command numbered, all told, 153—infantry, cavalry and teamsters—and ninety-six horses, including twenty teams taken along to carry camp and garrison equipage, rations and ammunition, and to transport our wounded, either soldiers or citizens. The expedition was under the immediate command of Captain H. P. Grant, of Company A. Major Joseph R. Brown, better known as "Old Joe Brown," was in charge of the scouts. He had a cool head, but no fighting qualities; had been an Indian trader for many years, raised an Indian family, and knew a great deal about Indian signs and customs. In this particular case, however, the Indians fooled Joe. The first day out we found and buried about fifty citizens, and at night went into camp in the river bottom near Redwood Crossing. The night was dark and dismal, and particularly sad to us

DR. WILLIAMSON'S HOUSE.

who had been gathering up the dead all day long. The instructions to the guard by Captain Anderson were of a very solemn nature, in view of the surroundings and the probable fighting ahead. This, together with the stillness of the night and the impression that a lurking foe was near, made the boys feel rather uncomfortable.

Deep sleep settled upon the camp, but the sentinels maintained a vigilant watch, however, and the night slowly passed without incident. After reveille the next morning we found Captain Marsh and his comrades, but not one of them answered to "roll-call." We found the captain's body and those of a few of his men in the river, and the rest of the bodies in the thicket on the river bank, where they had evidently been hemmed in and fired upon from all sides. Nearly all had been scalped, and were minus guns and ammunition, for these had been confiscated by the redskins. We buried the soldiers side by side, with their captain at their head, and marked the place by a huge cross, so that the bodies might be easily found and removed, which was subsequently done, when they were finally buried in the Soldiers' cemetery at Fort Ridgely. After this last service to our dead comrades, we took up the line of march, leaving the bottom lands for the prairie above, and it was when passing over the bluff that a large body of Indians, who were on their way to capture Saint Peter and Mankota, espied us. What was our subsequent loss was the gain of the two towns mentioned. Our scouts had crossed the river, making a detour to the south, and thus missed making the acquaintance of our enemies, who had their eyes on us.

We went into camp the second night near Birch Coolie, and sixteen miles distant from Fort Ridgely, about 5 p. m., well tired out with our day's march. Birch Coolie is a deep gorge running north and south in Redwood county, Minnesota. What was then a bleak prairie is now a beautiful farming community, and Birch Coolie a thriving village.

From information gathered by the scouts we felt comparatively safe.

Old Joe said: "Boys, go to sleep now and rest; you are as safe as you would be in your mother's house; there is not an Indian within fifty miles of you." At that very

"Chickens for Supper."

moment five hundred Indians were in the immediate vicinity watching us and impatient for the ball to open, as they intended it should at the proper time, which, with the Indian, is about four o'clock in the morning.

After our supper on chicken stew, song-singing and story-telling, we turned in, well tired out and in a condition to enjoy a good night's sleep and dreams of home.

The night was warm, the sky clear, with the stars shining

brightly, and a full moon in all her glory. It was a beautiful night—too beautiful to witness the scene that was so soon to follow. The guard had been stationed and cautioned to be on the alert for strange sounds; "tattoo," "roll-call," "taps," sounded, and the little camp was silent. The low hum of voices became less and less as slumber came to the weary soldiers, and all that could be heard was the occasional challenge of the guard: "Halt! who comes there!" as he was being approached by the officer of the guard.

Soon the soldiers slept, little dreaming that the lurking enemy and death were so near. The awakening to some was in eternity.

CHAPTER XVIII.

BATTLE OF BIRCH COOLIE.

The battle of Birch Coolie was fought September 2 and 3, 1862. It has never taken its proper place in history, but with the exception of the massacre at the Little Big Horn, in 1876, it was the hottest and the most desperate battle fought during the war of the Rebellion or any of our Indian wars. In comparison to the number of men and horses engaged, I know of no conflict, the one above referred to excepted, where the casualties were as great as they were here.

The Indian custom is to make an attack about four o'clock in the morning, so this relief had been especially cautioned, and soon after the guard was placed one of them thought he saw something moving in the grass. It proved to be an Indian, and they were slowly moving in upon us, their intention being to shoot the pickets with arrows, and as noiselessly as possible rush in and destroy us in our confusion. The sentinel fired at the moving object, and instantly our camp was encircled by fire and smoke from the guns of five hundred Indians, who had hemmed us in. The guard who fired escaped the bullet intended for him. He said he thought the moving object in the grass might be a hog or it might be an Indian, and, hog or Indian, he intended to kill it if he could. The fire was returned by the pickets as they retreated to the camp, and although there necessarily was confusion, there was no panic. Quicker than I can write we were out, musket in hand, but the captain's command to "fall down" was mistaken for "fall in," which makes a vast difference under such circumstances. We soon broke for the wagons, however, which were formed in a circle about our tents, and this afforded us some little shelter.

As this was our baptismal fire, and a most important engagement, I devote more space to it than I otherwise would. What an experience it was to inexperienced, peaceable, unsuspecting men! Think of being awakened out of a blissful sleep by the fire from five hundred Indian rifles—it is a wonder that we were not all destroyed amid the confusion that naturally would follow; but we had cool heads among us, and none were cooler than Old Joe Brown and Captain H. P. Grant, of Company A, who was in immediate command. I will here refer to two others. First, Mr. William H. Grant, a lawyer of St. Paul, who still lives in Minnesota. He went out to see the fun. Well, he saw it, and the "trial" was a severe one. He "objected" and "took exceptions" to everything the Indians did.

He wore a black plug hat, and this was a good mark for the redskins; they shot it off his head twice, and it was finally lost altogether. "Bill" was cool; he did not lose his temper, but laid down very flat on the ground and gave directions to those about him how to shoot to kill. We afterward voted him in as a brevet private, and were always ready to divide grub and "shake." Postmaster Ed. Patch, of St. Anthony, was another of our citizen escorts. He was a jolly good fellow and "cool as a cucumber," with a bay window on him like an overgrown bass drum. He found this excess of stomach very much in the way, in his great desire to hug mother earth and get out of range of the Indian bullets, and looked as if he wished he had never been born, or that he had been a disciple of anti-fat.

One of our little thin fellows was lying down alongside of "Ed," and I'll never forget the expression of his face when he said: "God, bub, I wish I was as little as you be."

The camp was miserably located, being commanded by the deep ravine on one side and by a mound on the other, so that the savages were well sheltered from our fire. Had the instructions given by Colonel Sibley been followed, which were always to encamp in open and level prairie, there would have been no such destruction of valuable lives, but the spot was chosen for our camp because it was near wood and water, and the Indians were supposed to be fifty miles away. It was a mistake, which we discovered after it was too late. A brisk fire was opened by the boys, and soon the cartridge boxes were being depleted. Ammunition was called for, and upon opening a box, to our dismay we found it to be of too large a calibre. Other boxes were opened with a like result. In loading up our ammunition a mistake had been made, and we found ourselves in this unfortunate dilemma; but no time was to be lost, as we had not more than an average of twenty rounds to the man, and a hoard of savages about us who seemed well supplied with powder and ball.

We went to work cutting the large bullets down with our knives, but this was a slow and unsatisfactory process. We used the powder from these large cartridges to load our guns with, putting in an extra amount, so that when we fired these blanks they made a great noise, and thus kept up a successful "bluff," though doing no damage. A dead silence would ensue, and occasionally some of our best shots picked off a more daring redskin simply to remind them that we were awake. We had but one shovel and one pick; there were others in some of the wagons, or they had been thrown out in the grass and could not be found. The captain offered $5 apiece for them, but the bullets were too thick to admit of a search, so we used jack-knives, spoons and bayonets to dig our intrenchments with. In time we had very good pits dug, and with the assistance of the dead bodies of our horses had ourselves tolerably well protected.

With the wounded horses rearing and plunging, the men groaning and calling for help, the hurried commands, and the unearthly yells of the five hundred red devils about us, this baptismal fire was trying to the souls of raw recruits, as most of us were. We were encircled by fire and smoke, the bullets were doing their deadly work, and it really seemed as though no man could escape death. Our orders were: "Load and fire, but steady, boys, and give them hail Columbia!"

Upon the first fire of the Indians two men fled from the camp, one a citizen, who was with us, and the other a soldier. The citizen we found afterward on the prairie, dead. He was the last of his family, for we had buried his wife and two children just the previous day, before going into camp. The soldier, a Swede, returned, but he was so paralyzed with fear that he was like a dead man during all this memorable thirty-six hours, and the poor fellow afterward succumbed to sickness. Everything was improvised for a barricade—camp kettles, knapsacks, wagon-seats, etc., and it was done in a hurry, for hot work was on our hands. The word soon went the rounds: "College is dead, Irvine is dead, Baxter, Coulter, Benecke, King and a score of others are dead, and nearly all are wounded." It was only a few minutes after the first fire when we realized all this, and it verily looked as though the little command would be wiped out of existence. If a head was shown fifty Indians leveled at it. During all this terrible fire Old Joe Brown walked about seemingly unconcerned, until a bullet went through the back of his neck. He came to the ground as quick as if shot through the heart, for it was a bad wound, but with it all he continued to give instructions. Nearly all the damage was done before ten o'clock, for up to that time we found ourselves with sixty killed and wounded, out of 155, and ninety-five horses dead, out of ninety-six. The horses saved our little encampment. As soon as they fell their bodies formed a good barricade for us, and this and the overturned wagons were our only protection. The Indians, occupying higher ground than we did, had us at a disadvantage. The day wore on, and all we could do was to assist Surgeon J. W. Daniels with the wounded and keep the Indians at bay. Dr. Daniels proved himself a cool-headed, brave man, never flinching for a moment. Where duty called he was found, and he immortalized himself with the boys. The great fear of the wounded seemed to be that we would be obliged to abandon them to their fate, for the sun was extremely hot and the camp had become very offensive from the smell of decomposing bodies of horses; besides, we had no means of transporting the wounded, and their fears were not without foundation, for it looked as though we would be driven by necessity from the camp. We assured and reassured them that if we went they would go, too. If we died it would be in defending them as well as ourselves.

The one thing, aside from cowardice on the part of the Indians, that saved us from assault was the fact of our having several half-breed scouts with us, who talked back and forth.

The Indians said: "Come out from the pale-faces; we do not want to kill you, but we want all their scalps."

Private James Auge of our company was the spokesman. He was a Canadian Frenchman, but had lived among the Indians, knew them well, and spoke their language, and as he went so would all the other Indians and half-breeds who were with us.

CHAPTER XIX

BIRCH COOLIE CONTINUED.

On the second day, at about sunrise, we discovered a large body of Indians closing up nearer to us, when one of their number, probably Little Crow's brother, came within twenty rods of us. He was on a white horse, and carried a flag of truce. He held a conversation with Auge, our interpreter, and tried to persuade him to leave us and bring the other half-breeds with him. When the conversation was interpreted to Captain Grant, he said: "Well, Auge, what do you fellows intend to do, go with the Indians or stay with us?" Auge replied:

"Captain Grant, we want nothing to do with these Indians; we will stand by you and fight as long as there is a man left, and I will now tell them so." He did call to them, and said:

"We won't come over to you; we will stay with the soldiers, and if you come we will kill you if we can. You are cowards to kill poor women and children, and if we catch you we will treat you as you treated them."

We felt relieved to know that our half-breeds were loyal. Auge, after this, was Corporal Auge, and he went all through the South with us, making a splendid soldier. I

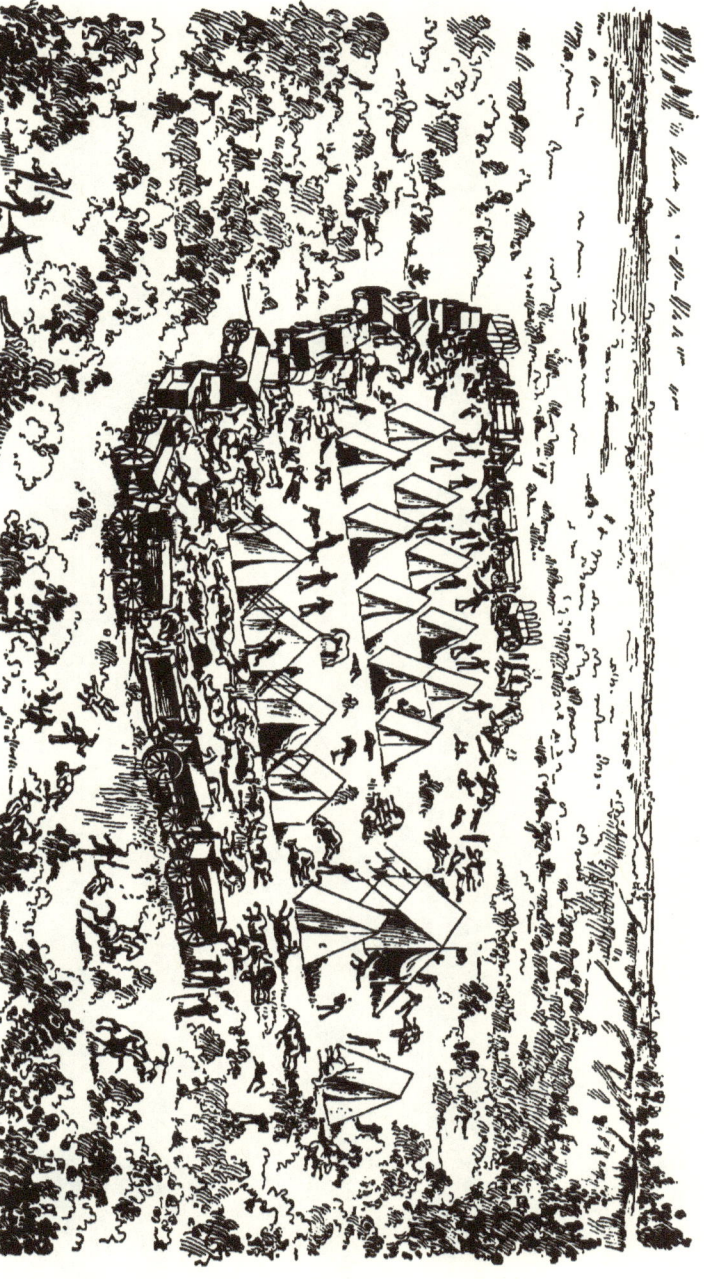

Designed by A. P. Connolly.

BATTLE OF BIRCH COOLIE, MINN.

Fought September 2nd and 3d, 1862. Ninety-five horses lay dead within the camp; 60 men killed and wounded; 500 Indians were under cover in the tall grass, and concentrated their fire on the camp.

shall have occasion to refer to him in another place in this chapter.

Captain Grant told Auge to say to them that we had two hundred fighting men and plenty of ammunition, and that Little Crow and all his dirty Indians could not take us, and for him to get out with his flag of truce.

It was a game of bluff, for at that time we only had about sixty-five effective men, and were nearly out of ammunition.

We did not know whether we could trust the half-breeds or not, and were instructed to fire on them to kill if they made the slightest move to desert us. Our firing had been heard at Fort Ridgely, sixteen miles away, and the Colonel dispatched two hundred and fifty men, with one howitzer, to our relief.

Just at sunset the second day we saw two horsemen come to the edge of the woods across the Coolie, but the Indians also saw them, and chased them back. They returned to their command and reported a large body of Indians, and said they saw a small camp with the stars and stripes flying, but as they had no field glass, could not make it out. Colonel McPhail, who was in command of this relief, ordered the howitzer to be fired to give us courage, if the little camp proved to be ours. A shout went up at this welcome sound just as the sun went down. Old Joe Brown, who had been disabled early in the day, called out from his tent: "Captain Grant, instruct the men to be watchful; we are in a bad fix; the Indians will hate to lose our scalps, now that they are so near their grasp; give them a few shots occasionally, assure the wounded men that we will not leave them, and keep the pick and shovel busy." We disposed of ourselves for the night as best we could.

Every man was on guard, and nearly all had two rifles fully charged and bayonets fixed. We clasped our rifles, looked up into the starry heavens, and, asking God's protection, swore not to yield an inch. We made this demonstration to encourage the wounded men, who seemed fearful that something more terrible was in store for them. The prayers and groans of the wounded and the awful silence of the dead inspired us to do our whole duty. The watch-word, "wide-awake," went the rounds every few minutes, and there was "no sleep to the eye nor slumber to the eye-lids," during all that live-long night.

Out of our ninety-six horses we had but one left. This was a splendid animal, and had thus far escaped without a scratch. He was feeding about the camp, unmindful of the fate of his fellows.

The picture of Birch Coolie is an exact reproduction of the situation. The ninety-five dead horses were all within the enclosure, and the one who escaped for the time is grazing among them.

Just before midnight the clouds began to gather, and we felt cheered to think we would soon have rain. We were sorely in need of water, for we had not tasted a drop since the night before, and the wounded men were nearly famished with thirst and burning with fever. As the sky darkened Captain Grant called for a volunteer to go to Fort Ridgely for relief. Corporal James Auge volunteered to go, and by this act proved himself a truly brave man, and if it had been successfully carried out would have gained for him a commission at no very distant day. The fact of its not being carried out was no fault of his, and, in the abandonment of the trial, he was declared not the less brave by all his comrades, who trembled for him while he was preparing to make the perilous journey. The night was cloudy, and he being conversant with Indian methods and well posted in the topography of the country, could be successful in getting through the Indian's lines, if anybody could; but the chances were ten to one against the success of the undertaking.

The horse was saddled and the Corporal had his instructions. He had his foot in the stirrup when the clouds rolled back from the full moon like the rolling back of a scroll, and it was almost as light as noonday. The Indians, ever on the alert, saw the preparations and opened fire anew upon us, and, long before they ceased, our good horse was pierced by six bullets, and the project was abandoned—we could only wait anxiously for results. The enemy did not allow us to wait long, for at four o'clock they opened a terrific fire, which they kept up for an hour. The only response they got from us was blank cartridges, but we made a great noise with them, and it answered the purpose very well. We had ourselves so well protected that in this fusilade they killed but one man and wounded another.

The early morning dawn and heavy, dewy atmosphere found our eyes heavy from loss of sleep, so we divided up and some slept while others watched. We heard nothing of the detachment, and as the day advanced the Indians became bolder. They had driven the relief back and were closing in upon us, and we, having so little ammunition, could do them but little harm. They were puzzled at our silence. Some of the chiefs said it was a trick, others said we were all killed. At any rate, with them "discretion was the better part of valor," and we didn't object.

About one o'clock the same day we descried the glimmer of the polished rifle in the distance. We had no glass, but anxious eyes strained to see what it was, and the dark outline of a moving mass told us reinforcements were coming. The chiefs, by waving their blankets and shouts, called off their warriors. "There's a mile of whites coming," they said. They waved their tomahawks, shouted, fired, and finally galloped off on the prairie.

A few warriors more daring than the others remained behind for a time to get a scalp, and some of them came so close we could readily discern their war paint. Before the main body of the Indians left, however, they rode very close, and gave us several parting volleys. The wounding of a few of our men was all the damage they did at this time.

Right joyful were we when the reinforcements arrived. Our camp had been formed by driving twenty teams in a circle, and it can readily be seen that it was not large. It was about as large as an ordinary circus tent, and inside of this we had our horses, men and tents. After the battle the sight was a sickening one, for with sixty dead and wounded men and ninety-five horses in such a small space, and all the confusion arising out of such a siege it was enough to appall the stoutest heart. Strong men, when they beheld the sight, wept like children. It was our baptismal fire, and the horror seemed greater to us. Our men, whose nerves had been on a tension so long and bodies exhausted for want of food, water and sleep, when the relief came, fell down and slept. Colonel Sibley was the first to arrive, and when he rode up to our barricade, and saw the terrible loss of life he looked as though he had lost his best friends. His heart bled at the sight, and the tears he shed spoke volumes. A detail was at once made to bury the dead side by side in a temporary grave, dinner was cooked for the remainder of the command and the wounded were put in ambulances, tents were "struck," and we took up the line of march for Fort Ridgely, which we reached sometime during the night. Our tents had been so completely riddled with bullets that they were condemned as useless, and were finally sent down to Fort Snelling and placed on exhibition for a long time. One of them had 375 bullet holes in it, and when the people looked at them they wondered that any man escaped. The narrow escapes were almost miraculous, and congratulations were frequently in order. It was not every man for himself, but a strong fellow-feeling sprang up among us that forever afterwards cemented our hearts. We shared our shelter and encouraged one another, and no man shrank from duty. We had determined to die together, and if ever soldiers stood shoulder to shoulder we did on this bloody spot, where our nerves and courage were taxed to the utmost. Company A, so nearly wiped out, was ever afterwards considered the "Old Ironsides" of the regiment.

Before we left, Colonel Sibley addressed a note to Little Crow, and placing it on a stick stuck it in the ground so he might find it when he would visit the battle ground, as he surely would do as soon as we were out of the way. The note was as follows:

"If Little Crow has any proposition to make let him send a half-breed to me and he shall be protected in and out of my camp.   H. H. Sibley,
            Colonel Commanding Military Expedition.

To specify the remarkable escapes would unduly lengthen this chapter, but, as near as my recollection serves me, no man entirely escaped. I'll specify two—one an escape and the other an incident. Lieutenant Swan, of the Third Minnesota, now a lawyer of Sioux City, Iowa, was with us on this picnic. He was not ordered to go, neither was he detailed, but he simply went, and he had a very narrow escape. During the sharp firing, and after we had some shallow pits dug, this officer was in one as far as his long legs would admit. He had a fine gold watch in his fob pocket, and one of the boys asked him the time of day. He undoubled as well as he could and got out his watch, but in returning it put it in his vest pocket instead of the fob. It was no sooner in his pocket than an Indian bullet struck it squarely in the center. The concussion knocked the lieutenant over, but the watch saved his life. He keeps it as a valued souvenir of the occasion.

The incident relates to Private James Leyde, of Company A, of the Sixth. He was a little fellow who could march longer and eat oftener than any youngster of his size I ever saw. Jimmy was a splendid soldier, always ready for drill or guard, and never forgot his manners when he met a "shoulder-straps." He was a pious little fellow, too, and carried a Bible his mother gave him.

Well, "after the battle" Jimmy was looking over the wreck with his comrade, Billy Caine, and in taking up his Bible found a bullet embedded in it. "Hello, Billy, my Bible got struck!" The ball had gone through Genesis, Exodus and Leviticus, until it stopped half way through Deuteronomy. Jimmy says: "God, Billy, it didn't get through Deuteronomy anyway!"

There were many close calls, and it really seemed remarkable that so many could escape. I could specify scores, but it is not necessary.

Among the incidents on the march before we arrived

at Birch Coolie I might mention the finding of a wounded woman by the roadside. She had been without food or water for twelve days, and was the only one of a large party supposed to have been murdered. She did not escape uninjured, however, for the surgeon took fourteen buckshot from her back. During our thirty-six hours' siege this poor woman remained in the wagon where she had been placed the first day, and spent her time in praying for our deliverance. She sustained a broken wrist in addition to her other wounds, but after we got to the fort she was among her own people and soon fully recovered to tell the tale of her twelve days' wanderings and her marvelous escape.

CHAPTER XX.

BATTLE OF WOOD LAKE.

At this juncture the press and people were clamoring for Colonel Sibley's removal because of his delay and, as they claimed—lack of energy and judgment. He lacked in neither, for he knew the foe he had to deal with, and if he had heeded the behests of the press and people, so far away, not a woman or child of the captives would have escaped. However, he dispatched Col. William Crooks to St. Paul to explain the situation in detail to Governor Ramsey and satisfy the clamorous press that they knew but little of the situation as it existed at the seat of the Sioux war.

After our return to Fort Ridgely and a few more days of preparation, the command was put in splendid marching condition, and "forward" was the word for the rescuing of the captives and if possible the capture of the renegades. We met the Indians next at Wood Lake and had a sharp battle with them early in the morning. They had come down in force to annihilate us, but we were glad to meet them in broad day light on the open prairie and receive them with "open arms to hospitable graves." We were just up from a good night's sleep and had partaken of a generous supply of Old Java and "hard tack," and felt

Designed by A. P. Connolly.

BATTLE OF WOOD LAKE, MINN.

Fought September 23d, in which the Indians were defeated.

abundantly able to defend ourselves. Besides we were veterans now, for we had profited by our baptismal fire and had an old score to settle with "Mr. Injun," and we settled to our entire satisfaction.

Our sappers had gone out to repair a bridge that had been burned, and the temptation was too great for some of the younger warriors. The plan of the Indians was to surprise us as we were crossing the river—to divide our attention by having a small body in the rear and one in front, and then the main body to spring from their ambush, and in our confusion to destroy us; but the young bucks, when they saw a few of our men, wanted their scalps so bad they opened fire. The "long roll" was sounded, and we stood to arms. Little Crow knew that Colonel Sibley was aware of his tactics, and was determined to remove him if he could by detailing about eighty of his best warriors to do the work, and at this battle of Wood Lake they tried hard to reach him, but he was too watchful to be caught napping. A detachment of the Third Minnesota, under Major Welch, and the Renville Rangers charged upon the Indians in one direction, and the Seventh Minnesota, in command of Col. William R. Marshall, in another, while the battery, under command of Captain Mark Hendricks, did effective work also. The Sixth Minnesota, under command of Colonel William Crooks, routed the Indians from a deep ravine on the right flank of our camp and probably saved Colonel Sibley from being captured by the picked men sent out for that purpose by Little Crow.

The conflict lasted more than two hours and was decisive. The Indians offered to surrender if Colonel Sibley would promise them immunity from punishment, but this was sternly refused. They fled in dismay, not being permitted to take their dead and wounded from the field. So confident were they of success that they had brought their women and teams to take back the pillage after the Indians had loaded themselves with glory and scalps—but presto, change; they got no glory and lost their scalps.

The soldiers had not forgotten Birch Coolie quite so soon and took great pleasure in procuring Indian scalps for trophies.

"Other Day," who guided a large party in escaping the massacre, seemed to have a charmed life, and a little incident here, in which he is the chief figure, will not be amiss. "Other Day," the same as other scouts, wore United States clothing. The day before the Wood Lake battle he was out scouting, and coming to a house turned his pony out to graze and lay down to take a noon-day nap. An Indian espied the pony and wanted it. He stealthily came up to the sleeping "Other Day," and putting up some kind of a sign so he might know a brother Indian had his pony, he rode off with the animal. "Other Day," considerably crestfallen, came back to headquarters and reported his loss and the manner of it. The Colonel and his staff had a hearty laugh at his expense, which rather offended his Indian sensitiveness. "Never mind," says he, "me get two for one."

Early next morning "Other Day" put on his Indian toggery, paint, feathers and all, and as the Indians hove in sight the morning of the Wood Lake battle, he started out on his pony hunt. Our men espied him across the ravine, and thinking him a hostile opened fire on him. His blanket was perforated with bullets, even the feathers in his hair were shot off, and yet no harm came to him. After the battle he came in with two ponies, and reporting to the Colonel, laughingly said: "Me got two for one." His wonderful escape was the talk of the camp, and the Colonel had an order issued prohibiting any one attached to the command, in the future, wearing anything but the United States regulation uniform.

The battle was a very decisive one and very discouraging to the Indians, who suffered a loss of 175 in killed and wounded, while our loss was fifty-seven killed and wounded. The engagement lasted two hours, and after the dead were gathered up and buried and the wounded cared for the column was again ready to move. This battle developed the fact that the Indian forces resisting our advance were composed in part of the Medawakantons and Wahpekutas of the Lower and Wahpetons and Sissetons of the Upper Sioux and Winnebagos, half-breeds and deserters from the Renville Rangers.

The utmost solicitude was expressed for the safety of the white prisoners, who knew that the Indians had gone down to fight the soldiers. They knew the temper of the squaws especially and feared the results of the battle. They heard the firing of the howitzer away in the distance, and by noon squaws began to arrive and in a most unhappy mood.

It was immediately after the battle of Wood Lake that General Pope wrote to General Halleck as follows;

"You do not seem to be aware of the extent of the Indian outbreak. The Sioux, 2,600 warriors, are assembled at the Upper Agency to give battle to Colonel Sibley, who is advancing with 1,600 men and five pieces of artillery. Three hundred and over of women and children are captives in their hands. Cannot the paroled officers and men of the rifle regiment (dragoons) now in Michigan be sent here?"

The stay-at-homes, who were loudest in their complaints, were raising the cry, "On to Richmond," on the one hand, and then again, "On to Little Crow" on the other. Colonel Sibley stood like a man of iron against these impatient behests. The "howlers" were not heeded, and in the liberation of the captives he gained the gratitude of the nation and a merited promotion.

The friendly chiefs who had determined at all hazards to protect the defenseless women and children redoubled their vigilance during the night; because they, too, knew the temper of a vanquished Sioux warrior. The position of these poor creatures was truly pitiable.

No less than four different councils were convoked, the Upper Indians arrayed, in a measure, against the Lower, and a quarrel ensued. Little Paul, Red Iron, Standing Buffalo, Chaska and a hundred Sissetons determined to fight Little Crow himself should any attempt be made to massacre the captives or place them in front at the coming battle. The hostiles began to fear that judgment was near, and it compelled Little Crow to assume a spirit of bravado not at all in consonance with his feelings.

Colonel Sibley, when he came in sight of the hostile camp, did not do as the majority of the soldiers thought he ought; viz., march up and at once surround the camp. This is where his coolness and knowledge of the Indians served him so good a purpose. He knew if he attempted such a course that the renegade Indians in the camp would at once take the alarm and run away, and that probably before they did go they would attempt to take the prisoners with them, and failing in this would kill them outright.

INDIAN CAMP TAKEN BY COLONEL SIBLEY.

He was informed of this by one of the scouts and at once concluded to adopt but one course, to go into camp and pay no attention to them and thus disarm them of any fear as to his real intention. While the Colonel did this, and apparently intended to leave them alone, he was informing himself of the condition of affairs in the Indian camp. He learned that several of the worst bands had gone farther up north, and he sent word to them to return and they should not be harmed. Several bands did come back, but there were those who did not, and after the scouts had located them, companies of soldiers were sent out to make their capture. In this way they all came back or were captured and compelled to come, excepting Little Crow and his immediate followers.

At Camp Release we attended to guard mount, company and battalion drill, and all other duties incident to a soldier's life. It became necessary to make a concerted move against the Indian camp in our immediate vicinity and relieve the white prisoners, and the orders were received one night for all the infantry to turn out at twelve midnight. It was to be done noiselessly, and the instructions were so given. The whole command marched out in single file until the Indian camp was surrounded, and then we were ordered to close in. After this was done we received orders to lie down and to remain until daylight, when, at the sound of reveille, we were to rise up. The Indians, hearing the early bugle call so near them, flocked out to see what it was and found themselves prisoners.

Negotiations at once commenced for the unconditional surrender of the white prisoners, and the object about which General Sibley was so solicitous was accomplished. He knew that he could not attack the hostiles in the friendly camp without endangering the lives of the captives, and that the best policy was to appear indifferent about their presence and thus disarm them of fear. The plan worked admirably, and the game was successfully bagged.

OTHER DAY.

CHAPTER XXI.

CAMP RELEASE.

Among the attractive and cultivated women found among the prisoners was a Miss Mattie Williams, of Painesville, Ohio, who at the time of the outbreak was living with an uncle on the Yellow Medicine River. They had been surprised by the Indians without a moment's warning, and of course, in their hurry, had no time to plan for an escape; but each sought safety as best they could and became separated. Miss Williams, in her wanderings, was picked up by a Mr. Patwell, who was escaping with a German girl, who also was fleeing. They were overtaken by the Indians, Mr. Patwell was killed, the German girl so wounded that she died, and Miss Williams herself, wounded in the shoulder, was alone with her Indian captors, who imposed upon her all the indignities born of their hellish desires. For forty days she suffered as no human mind can imagine, forty anxious days and sleepless nights in a dirty, smoke-begrimed, leaky tent, clad in Indian costume and obliged to submit to savage passion. But the angels listened and the day of deliverance drew near. The women of this camp were all of one mind—in accord they prayed that deliverance should come, and that the guiding hand should be directed by a clear head. As Moses was preserved in the bulrushes and found by Pharaoh's daughter and educated for a purpose—to lead the children of Israel from out the land of bondage and through the Red Sea to the wilderness and the promised land—so, too, was Colonel Sibley raised up to frustrate the designs of the Indians and liberate these women and children.

On the night of September 25th our heroine, wrapped in her Indian blanket, laid herself down, not to pleasant dreams, but to blissful waking visions of release. Nor was she alone in her night vigils; other hearts, burdened and borne down with unutterable anguish, petitioned God to so direct the soldiers who were on the way, that their release might be sure. The soldiers are coming, and are these weary, anxious, fearful days and nights to end? At the first dawning of the day, September 26th, the Indian camp was astir and preparations made to receive distinguished guests. And who were these guests? Colonel Sibley, the big white chief, and his staff. Extra paint, paint of every hue, and beads, together with eagle feathers and white flags, were conspicuous throughout this excited Indian tepee village.

The bright gleam of muskets away in the distance, banners fluttering in the breeze and the sound of martial music as it struck the glad expectant ear, was an answer to all their prayers: "Deliverance had come!" Hearts made glad because the terrible nightmare of weeks had been dissipated, the anxious days and sleepless nights were at an end, prayers had been answered, and it was now a time for thanksgiving. Was it ended, this horrible dream? Yes. But with it all, strong attachments sprang up between the captive and the captor. They would have been less than human if it were not so. These sturdy and determined

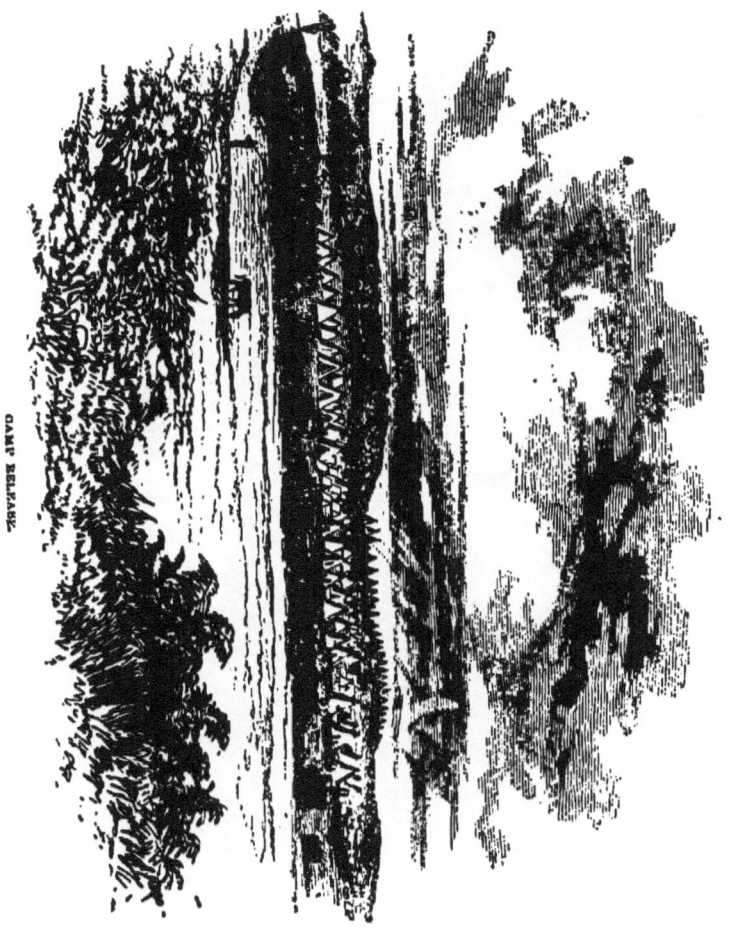

Indian women and men who protected them had jeopardized their lives, and what greater love can we show one for the other than that we lay down our lives?

The little children, from one year up to four or five, who had become orphaned, were adopted by the Indian mother, and these mothers, who became so under such sorrowful circumstances, and having all the maternal instincts of her more favored white sister, cared for them as tenderly as she did her own. The little things were there with their dirty, chubby faces, just the same as their Indian mates, their faces were painted, their hair braided and garnished with eagle feathers, and they really seemed happy and contented amid their changed and strange environments. When the time came for them to go to our camps they cried and wanted to stay with their newly found Indian mothers, and the mothers in turn hugged them and cried over them and hated to give them up. There is nothing passes a mother's love, even an Indian mother's love.

It was a proud day for Colonel Sibley, and as he looked into the happy faces of the captives and received their blessings and reverent homage, his heart was touched and tears coursed down his cheeks. He was yet a colonel, so far as we knew, and one of his staff officers, in addressing him said:

"Colonel Sibley, I would rather have the glory of your achievement to-day than the proudest victory ever won in battle."

The military camp at this point was designated Camp Release, so named from the nature of our mission in releasing the people from their Indian captivity. The manner in which they were rescued and the Indians captured reflects greatly to the credit and sagacity of Colonel Sibley and his advisers. The impetuous and indignant soldiers, after what their eyes had beheld in the region where the whites had been murdered, were determined to annihilate the camp, and it was almost impossible to restrain them, especially Company A, of the Sixth Minnesota, which had suffered so severely at Birch Coolie; but wiser counsels prevailed.

After the Indians had been secured, and the captives released, we went among them and listened to the recital of experiences that would make the blood of any ordinary mortal boil with indignation, and it was a miracle that the soldiers did not take the matter in hand and then and there forever settle the Indian question. The orders were very strict about guarding the Indians, but on the sly many acts of cruelty were indulged in by the soldiers that would hardly be warranted, for we should not for a moment forget the fact that they were our prisoners and we were not savages and should not indulge in savage propensities.

Colonel Henry Hastings Sibley at Camp Release received a notification of his deserved promotion, and we shall hereafter speak of him as General Sibley.

During our stay at Camp Release we were daily drilling by company and battalion, and perfecting ourselves in all things pertaining to soldier life. We had a splendid camping place on the broad prairie near the river bank, but the cold nights reminded us that winter quarters would soon be more comfortable than the open prairie, and the rations were getting rather scarce. "Fall in for grub" ordinarily is quite as welcome to the hungry soldier as is the gong at a fashionable hotel to the fashionable guest. How we jumped for the haversack containing, not solid silver, but tin cup, tin plate, knife, fork and spoon, and fell in line according to our agility to get there, and not according to size, so as to give the ponies an equal chance with the tall men, whose place is on the right when in parade. Each received his ration of coffee, hard tack, pork and beans, irrespective of size, weight or previous condition.

Commissary stores at Camp Release were getting very low and the supply train was not yet due by several days' march, so it became necessary to count out the crackers—five crackers to each man for a day, and no pie or strawberries and cream for dessert. From five we were reduced to three, and then there was nothing left but the bottom of the barrels. There was some ear corn, but a guard was placed over that to keep it safe for the horses and mules. Every mule was honored with a guard during his meal hour to prevent the "boys in blue" from appropriating the precious ear for his own use. No coffee, no meal, no hardtack, but there was a load of potatoes remaining, and when the call to grub sounded, again we scrambled into line to receive our ration for the day, which was—one potato. Just after we received this potato ration the commissary train hove in sight under strong guard with three days' rations, which were issued to the hungry soldiers, and the indications were that the command would soon move.

CHAPTER XXII.

THE INDIAN PRISONERS—THE TRIAL.

After liberating the captives it became necessary to at once proceed against the Indians, and to this end the General appointed a commission consisting of Colonel William Crooks, president; Lieutenant-Colonel William R. Marshall, Captains H. P. Grant, H. S. Bailey and Rollin C. Olin and Lieutenant I. V. D. Heard as recorder. The Indians were properly represented, and through an interpreter understood the nature of the charges brought against them.

The rescued white captives, as soon as possible, were sent under suitable escort to Fort Ridgely and then forwarded to their friends. As before narrated, some of them had formed quite strong attachments for their dusky protectors.

And it is not to be wondered at. Because a man's skin is red or black it does not follow that his heart is black. The blackest hearts the world's history ever recorded beat beneath the whitest breasts.

These friendly Indians were in a very small minority, succeeded in saving the lives of the captives. It was a watch by day and by night, and through a bold determination, that the few friendly ones succeeded in saving, as they

THE COURT-HOUSE OF THE MILITARY COMMISSION.

did, these captives, and they would be less than human if they did not form strong attachments for their dusky friends.

After the departure of the white captives, the Indian trial proceeded, but for good reasons the General concluded to move the camp down to the Lower Agency on the Red Wood River. The Indian camp, mostly made up of women and children, had been moved from Yellow Medicine to this place, where the trial still progressed.

It was really amusing to sit by and listen to the testimony given in by the Indians through their interpreter. They were nearly all like the white criminals of to-day—innocent. I will only record a few. Cut Nose, for instance, will be a fair example of others, who were as guilty wretches as ever escaped the immediate vengeance of an outraged people.

The bloody old chief tried to play the innocent by saying he was not in the battles to hurt anyone. He was most always there, but he was engaged in some innocent pastime, such as feasting on roast beef and green corn, while his comrades of the paint and feathers were killing people by the score. If he fired at all it was at random and nobody was hurt. He would steal, but that was for the benefit of his wife; she insisted upon his doing something towards the support of herself and their Indian kids; but as for killing anyone, oh! no, he could not think of that for a minute.

We have his picture here, and his looks are a "dead giveaway;" and, besides, twenty-seven murders were traced directly to him, and his protestation of "me good Injun" all went for nought. He was a notoriously bad Indian; he was so adjudged by the commission, who condemned him to death, and he finally dangled at one end of a hempen cord.

Another one, prematurely gray, thought this ought to be evidence in his favor, and others protested that they

CUT-NOSE.
Who killed twenty-seven persons, and was hanged.

were too weak to face fire; others, that their lives were threatened and they were compelled to go on the war path; others, that they slept while their more wakeful companions fought; and one old man who said he was fifty years old a great many years ago, thought he might be excused, but a boy swore straight against him and said, "I saw that man kill my mother," which solemn words settled the prisoner's fate.

This Indian was "Round Wind," but it was afterwards shown that he was not there and he was reprieved just before the day set for the execution.

Among the Indian prisoners were some who had been enlisted in the "Renville Rangers," and had deserted to their friends—our enemies. These rangers were all Indians and half-breeds, and it was largely from this fact that the Indians conceived the idea that all the white men had left the state and that the time was propitious for the Indians to strike to regain their territory.

It was proven conclusively that these men had been in all the battles, and at Wood Lake one of them had taken the first scalp, and this from an old man and a former comrade in his company. For this he received one of the two belts of wampum which had been promised by Little Crow as a reward for killing the first white man. These men all offered excuses, but the evidence was so overwhelmingly against them that they also were condemned to death.

It was necessary to make an indiscriminate capture of the Indians and then investigate their several cases to find out the guilty ones, because, there were many among them who no doubt had been compelled to participate in the fights we had with them at Birch Coolie and Wood Lake, and only kept with the hostiles from policy and to save the lives of the white people. To these and a good old squaw, well known in St. Paul and other parts of the Union as "Old Betz," over 400 persons owe their lives.

"Old Betz" has gone to her reward in the happy hunting grounds, having lived over seventy-five years. She was a good woman and a good friend to the early settlers of Minnesota. Others who were friendly to the whites and loyal to their great father at Washington were liberated, and the guilty placed under strong guard.

OLD BETZ.

CHAPTER XXIII.

CAPTURE OF RENEGADE BANDS—MIDNIGHT MARCH.

General Sibley was apprised by his scouts that there were several lodges of Indians up around Goose Nest Lake, and also near the mouth of the Lac-qui-Parle River, and he dispatched Lieutenant-Colonel Marshall with two hundred and fifty men (having six days' rations) to bring them in. The little expedition started at midnight. They did not find Indians at the point designated, but struck across the country, and by a forced march of forty-five miles, found two lodges. They took the young men prisoners, but the women and children were placed in charge of the old men and sent away with instructions to report at Camp Release, which they did in due time. Colonel Marshall heard of twenty-seven lodges at a place described as Two Wood Lake, but upon arriving there, found the place deserted, the enemy leaving behind for the benefit of other Indians, a sign indicating that they had left two days before. In order to catch them, the infantry were instructed to follow, while the cavalry, with a howitzer, pushed on as fast as possible, and about midnight on the 16th the detachment came up to the Indians, who, unsuspecting, were enjoying their sleep. The barking of the dogs awoke them, and they realized that something unusual was about to occur. Peering out through the opening of their tepees, they saw horsemen and at once suspected they were soldiers. The half-breed scouts called upon them to surrender and they would not be harmed. Some of the younger men started to run away, but they were overtaken and all made prisoners. In their conversation with the interpreter they said they would have given themselves up, but were afraid to do so. They said they knew that starvation stared them in the face, because a cold winter was at hand, their provisions were all gone, and that for the sake of their families they were glad to be caught. They said also that Little Crow and some of his immediate followers had gone farther north, near Devil's Lake.

The game having been successfully bagged, Colonel Marshall hastened with the prisoners back to Camp Release, where everything was in readiness for a move down to Red Wood.

Among the Indians was a negro by the name of Godfrey. He had never known any other people and was totally ignorant concerning his parentage; but he was among them, taking part in all their battles, and a very active part, too, for the charge against him was "murder," in that with his own hand he had killed seven white men, women and children. He said he was not guilty. It is often thus—guilty men are innocent in their own estimation. Mr. O-ta-kle (Godfrey), was in his own opinion one of this sort. Certain it was, he had been enthusiastic over the prospect of the excitement that would follow a general uprising, for he put on a breech-clout and decorated his black face and legs in all the gorgeous hues of Indian war paint. He could "whoop" as loud and yell as fiercely as the best of them, and when the Indians returned from one of their raids he was accounted one of the bravest of their warriors. He admitted that he had killed seven; this he did, however, to his Indian comrades, when it would, if a fact, add feathers to his coronet and renown to his cruel record; but, when confronted by the men who could pass judgment against him if found guilty, he was the most innocent creature in all the world. In his hesitating, broken way of speaking, he gave a minute account of his whereabouts. There was no direct evidence against him, excepting his own confession to his comrades that he was with the Indians in all their raids and that he had killed seven people. In his earnest denial of the fact, he had such an honest look, and spoke with such a truthful tone, that the court, although prejudiced against him, were inclined to listen to his story with a reasonable degree of favor; yet he was finally found guilty and sentenced to be hanged, the verdict being accompanied with a recommendation that his punishment be commuted to imprisonment for ten years. He did not go to prison, but was sent to a reservation and compelled to stay there. Who he was, or where he came from, no one seemed to know, and he could remember nothing beyond his life among the Indians.

CHAPTER XXIV.

HOMEWARD BOUND.

"Reveille."

"We start for home to-morrow morning," were the gladsome words passed around the camp-fire on the evening of the 22d of October. The nights were getting chilly, and the shortening days indicated that the autumn was fast passing away, and that warmer quarters than our tents would soon be an absolute necessity. The contemplation of the homeward march was a pleasure, for there were ties of friendship there that forbade procrastination. A sad thought came over us as we remembered the poor fellows who had given up their lives—their waiting ones at home would wait in vain.

Reveille sounded early one morning, and after a hurried

breakfast of coffee and hard tack, the headquarters bugle sounded "strike tents," and the city of canvas was soon razed to the ground. With the captives and prisoners we took up our line of march for Yellow Medicine, where the commission appointed by the General tried and condemned 305 Indians to hang.

The morning we left Camp Release the sun shone brightly, the sky was clear, but there was frost in the air; and, as we were on very short rations and only one blanket each, we were in high glee as we marched out to the music of the band. I think our steps were more than the regulation twenty-eight inches, for we were headed towards God's country—home. About four p. m. the fierce fall wind veered around in our faces, and coming as it did off the burnt prairie, our faces soon presented the appearance of men from the interior of Africa. We were black in the face. At five o'clock we went into camp. It was pitch dark, with the wind blowing a hurricane, and in the darkness, infantry, cavalry, and artillery were one interminable mass of troops and order was impossible. So the orders were: "By company, left wheel, halt;" "stack arms;" "break ranks," with orders to pitch tents and get under cover. To make fires and cook supper was impossible, so we supped on raw salt pork, hard tack, and cold water. The Sibley tents blew down as fast as put up, and in this condition we crawled under them to get the best protection possible from the fierce northern blast. Some of the men had found potato cellars that had been dug in the hillside by the Indians, and taking possession of them were thus afforded good, warm quarters and plenty of potatoes to eat. In this respect they were much more fortunate than the rest of us who were on the outside and had all we could do to keep from freezing to death. The storm abated somewhat by morning, so we could make our fires, which we did, and availed ourselves of the Indian potatoes, and with salt pork, hard tack and coffee made a hearty breakfast and were soon on the march again.

The exposure of that night gave many of us the rheumatism, and it took several hours' march to get ourselves limbered up, but the day was bright and we were homeward bound. We made a good day's march, and pitched our tents in the valley of the Red Wood.

The Indian camp, consisting principally of women and children, had been previously removed to this place from Yellow Medicine, where the quartermaster had erected a large board prison to hold the captive red men, who had all been condemned by the Commission. The papers had been sent on to President Lincoln for his final decision, and we were here awaiting developments.

The condemned Indians were sent under strong guard to Camp Sibley, on the banks of the Red Wood River. They were chained together and kept in a structure built for the purpose, and their squaws, who were camped on the outside, were allowed to cook for them under the supervision of a guard, to prevent them from smuggling knives or a weapon of any kind on the inside of the enclosure.

After a week or ten days we again took up the line of march to a destination known only to the General and his Staff, but which proved to be that the Seventh Minnesota, under Colonel William R. Marshall, should proceed with the prisoners to Mankato, and the Sixth Minnesota, under Colonel Crooks, should report at Fort Snelling for further orders. The two regiments marched together until we reached a point some way below New Ulm. Nothing of

importance took place until we reached this place. The General having heard that the citizens had determined to kill every redskin regardless of consequences if they could possibly get hold of them, took precaution against it. It was said that every house was supplied with hot water, hot soft soap and anything and everything that ingenuity could invent to inflict sudden and sure punishment, and death if possible, to those that had brought such woe to them. For this reason the General changed his course somewhat, and making a detour to the right, escaped the necessity or perhaps bloodshed, in trying to save his captives from the hands of this justly furious people. Men and women turned out en masse and hurling imprecations, flourishing butcher knives, table knives, and even scissors, axes, pitchforks—in fact, every sort of weapon—seemed determined to get at them, and abused soldiers and Indians alike because they were held at bay. They followed us for two or three miles before they became convinced that the General was determined at all hazards to uphold the supremacy of the government in protecting these blood-stained captives from the furies of a people who had suffered so much at the hands of some of their tribes in the murder of their innocent women and children.

At a point below New Ulm the command was divided, a portion taking all the condemned men to Mankato, and the balance of the command proceeding to Fort Snelling.

At Mankato, as the days wore away and there was some doubt as to what the final decision of President Lincoln would be, great fear was entertained that there would be a general uprising of the people, and an attempt made to override military and civil law by wresting the Indians from the soldiers and instituting a general massacre of them, irrespective of their guilt or innocence, but Colonel Stephen Miller, the post commander, having determined that law and not lawlessness should prevail, used the utmost vigilance to defeat any such undertaking.

CHAPTER XXV.

PROTESTS—PRESIDENT LINCOLN'S ORDER FOR THE EXECUTION.

The Indians did not seem to feel cast down; some in fact appeared rather to enjoy the situation; others, again, were more serious, and were probably speculating as to the probable outcome of the unfortunate condition of affairs. The soldiers did not relish the idea of guarding them, and one night a conspiracy, which I overheard, was formed to create a false alarm in the camp and in the excitement fall on the Indians and murder them. The plot leaked out and the plan miscarried, as it should, for it would have been rank murder to have executed it. Among the prisoners there were many who really were not guilty, but had been caught in bad company. The prisoners were arraigned upon written charges specifying the criminating acts, and these charges were signed by General Sibley, and with but few exceptions were based on information furnished by Rev. S. R. Riggs, who had long been a missionary among them. The majority of the prisoners were condemned to death, and the news reaching the East, far away from the scene of the outrages, petitions went in from many New England cities, imploring the President to exercise clemency toward this unfortunate people. He yielded to the clamor in so far as only to include the very worst characters among them.

Bishop Whipple said: There are times when the Christian laborer has a right to ask for the sympathy, the prayers and the co-operation of our fellow-citizens, and to make a strong appeal in behalf of this most wretched race of heathen men on the face of the earth. The responsibility," he says, "is great, the fearful issues are upon us, and as we are to settle them justly or unjustly we shall receive the blessing or curse of Almighty God. Many of these victims of savage ferocity were my friends. They had mingled their voices with mine in prayer; they had given to me such hospitality as can only be found in the log cabin of the frontier; and it fills my heart with grief, and blinds my eyes with tears, when I think of their nameless graves. It is because I love them and would save others from their fate that I ask that the people shall lay the blame of this great crime where it belongs, and rise up with one voice to demand the reform of the atrocious Indian system, which has always garnered for us the same fruit of anguish and blood.

Thousands of miles away from the scene of the outrages perpetrated against the inoffensive white settlers, protests were sent in to the President from all sorts of humanitarians, imploring him to stay the sentence that condemned to death so many human beings. The provocation to indiscriminately condemn and hang was very great, for thousands of innocents had been ruthlessly murdered; no moments of warning were given them; no former kindnesses seemed to be remembered by the Indians, and their hands were steeped in their friends' blood, and there seemed no palliating circumstances. The enormity of the outbreak and the fiendish cruelty of the redskins were appalling; the people were paralyzed with astonishment and fear, and the witnesses, no doubt mistaken and prejudiced, gave such

INTERIOR OF INDIAN JAIL.

positive testimony that the commission felt satisfied in pronouncing them guilty of murder in the first degree; but would this have been the case if these prisoners had been white instead of red?

No doubt General Sibley himself was surprised when he learned of the indiscriminate condemnation of these prisoners, and was glad not to be held responsible for their hanging.

It is a fact that there were Indians found with arms in their hands in nearly all the battles, but their object was to protect the women and children prisoners, and they said they must make a show of fighting whether they did or not in order to accomplish this. It would have been a great stain on the fair name of our country if this wholesale hanging had occurred, and President Lincoln acted wisely in overruling the recommendation of the commission, which he did to such an extent as to sanction the execution of thirty-nine of the condemned men, and the balance to be further held as prisoners until he should designate a reservation to which they should be sent. During the time the preparations were being made to carry out the President's order the people were clamorous. They were not satisfied with the modification of the President's order, and grave rumors were abroad that there would be a vigorous effort made to take the Indians from the soldiers and have a wholesale execution, but the military authorities prevented it.

The President acted wisely in this matter. In fact, the state of the public mind was such and the pressure within our lines was exercised to such a degree that the President could do nothing less. If all the condemned Indians had been executed the impression would have gone abroad that the great government of the United States was putting to death its prisoners of war, and this would have done much toward bringing about a recognition of the Southern Confederacy.

The President's order was as follows:

"Executive Mansion,
"Washington, December 6, 1862.

"Brigadier-General H. H. Sibley, St. Paul, Minn.:

"Ordered, that the Indians and half-breeds sentenced to be hanged by the military commission, composed of Colonel Crooks, Lieutenant-Colonel Marshall, Captain Grant, Captain Bailey and Lieutenant Olin, and lately sitting in Minnesota, you cause to be executed on Friday, the 19th day of December, instant.

"The other condemned prisoners you will hold subject to further orders, taking care that they neither escape nor are subjected to any unlawful violence.

"Abraham Lincoln,
"President of United States."

The execution was carried out on the 26th of December, 1862. Thirty-eight were hanged.

CHAPTER XXVI.

THE EXECUTION—THE NIGHT BEFORE.

The date of the execution was fixed for December 26, 1862. On the 22d instant the condemned prisoners were separated from the others, and on the same day Colonel Stephen Miller (afterwards Governor), who was in command, through the interpreter, Rev. Mr. Riggs, called upon the condemned and announced the decision of the Great Father at Washington. He said:

Tell these thirty-nine condemned men that the commanding officer of this place has called to speak to them on a serious subject this afternoon. Their Great Father at Washington, after carefully reading what the witnesses testified to in their several trials, has come to the conclusion that they have been guilty of murdering his white children; and, for this reason, has directed that each be hanged by the neck until dead next Friday at ten a. m.

That good ministers, both Catholic and Protestant, are here, and can commune with them for the remaining four days they have to live.

That I will now cause to be read the letter from their Great Father at Washington, first in English and then in their own language.

Say to them, now, that they have so sinned against their fellow-men, that there is no hope for clemency except in the mercy of God, through the merits of the blessed Redeemer; and that I earnestly exhort them to apply to that, as their only remaining source of comfort and consolation.

Rev. Mr. Riggs, the interpreter, had been a missionary among them for twenty-five years, and he had known them intimately, and it pained him sorely to be obliged to convey to them as an interpreter the words that were to condemn them to death. In so doing he said:

I have known you for many years; I have pointed you to the cross; endeavored to prayerfully convince you that allegiance to God, and the Great Father at Washington, was your duty. I have with a broken heart witnessed your cruelty to inoffensive men, women and children; cruelty to your best friends. You have stained your hands in innocent blood, and now the law holds you to strict accountability. It pains me to inform you that your Great Father in Washington says you must die for your cruelty and murders, and I am directed to inform you that on the 26th day of February you will be hanged by the neck until you are dead, and may God have mercy on your souls.

The prisoners received the sentence rather coolly; some smoking their pipes composedly during its reading, one of them knocking the ashes out of his pipe, and another putting in his a fresh supply of Kinnikinick. On Tuesday evening they held a death dance, accompanied by wild Indian songs, and there were some fears that the excitement might cause an attempt to make an escape or create a panic; so, precautionary measures were taken. The Indians' friends and families were permitted to visit them and take a last farewell. It was a solemn time even to the white soldiers, for it was plainly evident that while there was a lack of such demonstration as would be witnessed among the whites under similar circumstances, yet to the observant eye only, it was plain to be seen that deep,

deep grief had taken possession of their hearts. There were few tears; no hysterics, but profound sorrow was depicted on the countenances as the parting word was said, and messages sent to children and friends. Some were completely overcome; others in bravado laughed and joked as if it were an every-day occurrence. One said: "Yes, tell our friends that we are being removed from this world over the same path they must shortly travel. We go first."

Many spoke in a mournful tone; in fact, the majority of them desired to say something, and with one or two exceptions they seemed to be penitent. Why should they not? Their white brethren under like circumstances are accorded religious privileges. They repent and accept the invitation, "Come unto Me all ye who are weary and heavy laden and I will give you rest." The thief on the cross repented. Could not an ignorant, misguided Indian under religious instruction receive light and repent?

The night before the execution Colonel Miller received a stay for one of the condemned, as strong doubt existed as to his participation in the murders, and he was finally pardoned.

It has been said that in the excitement of the preparations for the execution that the wrong man was pardoned. He was guilty, but the innocent man suffered in his stead. The last night was spent by the prisoners in quite a jolly camp-fire, chatting merrily and smoking to their hearts' content.

Father Ravoux, a Catholic priest from St. Paul, remained with them all night administering consolation and communion, and the more serious of them listened attentively to his words of comfort. In the morning, as the hour for the execution approached, and while Father Ravoux was speaking to the Indians, the provost marshal entered and whispered something to the good priest, who in turn spoke in French to one of the half-breeds, and he repeated it in Dakota to the Indians, who were all lying down around the prison. The information he gave was that the hour had arrived when they were to march to the gallows. In a moment every Indian stood erect, and as the provost marshal opened the door they fell in behind him with the greatest alacrity. Indeed, a notice of release, pardon or reprieve could not have induced them to leave their cells with more apparent willingness than this call to death. At the foot of the steps there was no delay. Captain Redfield mounted the drop, at the head, and the Indians crowded after him, as if it were a race to see who would get there first. They actually crowded on each other's heels, and as they got to the top, each took his position, without any assistance from those who were detailed for that purpose. They still kept up a mournful wail, and occasionally there would be a piercing scream. The ropes were soon arranged around their necks without the least opposition being offered. The white caps, which had been placed on the tops of their heads, were now drawn down over their faces, shutting out forever the light of day from their eyes. Then ensued a scene that can hardly be described and can never be forgotten. All joined in shouting and singing, as it appeared to those who were ignorant of the language. The tones seemed somewhat discordant, and yet there was harmony in it. It was not their voices alone, but their bodies swayed to and fro, and their every limb seemed to be keeping time. The drop trembled and shook as if all were dancing. The most touching scene on the drop was their attempt to grasp each other's hands, fettered as they were. They were very close to each other, and many succeeded. Three or four in a row were hand in hand, and all hands swaying up and down with the rise and fall of their voices. One old man reached out on each side, but could not grasp a hand; his struggles were piteous and affected many beholders.

Those who understood their manners and language said that their singing and shouting was necessary to sustain each other. Each one shouted his own name and called on the name of his friend, saying in substance: "I am here! I am here!"

The supreme moment arrived, and amid an immense concourse of citizens and soldiers the drop fell, and thirty-eight human beings, whose hands were steeped in innocent blood and who had spread such desolation and sorrow to thousands of happy homes, were ushered into the presence of their Maker.

The arrangements were under the immediate supervision of Captain Burt, of the Seventh Regiment, and they were so complete that there was not the slightest hitch.

"Positions of honor were given to the most interested. For instance, the cutting of the rope was assigned to William J. Daly, of Lake Shetek, who had three children killed and his wife and two children captured, and who were at this time in the hands of Little Crow, on the Missouri, and were afterward ransomed by Major Galpin at Fort Pierre."

The quotation I make here is from a book in the public library, and I found penciled on the margin by one of those persons who take advantage of the courtesies extended by public libraries, the following:

"So should every remaining Indian be 'elevated'!" Nay!

Nay! scribbler. We cannot tell why one man's face is black and another red, while yours and mine are white. Would you mete out the same measure to the whites? Innocency among the Indians, per capita, is not more rare than among their more favored white brethren, and we are brethren of a different hue. Punish the guilty, be he white or black, but protect the innocent.

After the bodies had hung for about half an hour, the physicians of the several regiments present examined them and reported that life was extinct. The bodies were carried away in United States mule teams and dumped in one common grave, dug in the sand bar in front of the city, the half-breeds in one corner of the hole so they might be found by their friends if they so desired. There may be times and circumstances when a Christian people can afford to act as we expect the benighted to do; but it has not arrived yet. No matter what the crime, the penalty has been paid, and after the spirit has gone to God to be adjudged, it is part of our civilization to be decent in our conduct toward all that remains mortal. It is not necessary to make a great display, but that we perform our duty according to our law. We have taken a life in accordance with a human law, and in justification of it we quote, "An eye for an eye and a tooth for a tooth." No matter how atrocious the deed, after the penalty has been paid we cannot as a Christian people, apologize for our acts of barbarism to the inanimate clay.

After the mandate of the President had been executed the telegraph flashed to Washington the following:

"St. Paul, Minn., December 27, 1862.
"To the President of the United States:
"I have the honor to inform you that the thirty-eight

Indians and half-breeds, ordered by you for execution, were hung on yesterday at Mankato, at ten a. m. Everything went off quietly, and the other prisoners are well secured.

"Henry H. Sibley,
"Brigadier-General."

With this the curtain drops on this bloody drama, and thus ended the great Indian campaign of 1862.

CHAPTER XXVII.

SQUAWS TAKE LEAVE OF THEIR HUSBANDS.

The condemned men, and the others who were to be deported after the execution took place, were called upon to bid good-bye to their wives and children, who were to be taken down to Fort Snelling. The wives were allowed a few at a time to go inside the jail and with the children have words of conversation with the husband and father. After a reasonable time they took leave of them. There were no hysterics, no sobs, no tears, but the heart-beats and the thoughts were there. Love? Yes. How deep, no white on-looker could tell. It was a supreme moment to the poor Indian and his dusky wife. Their roads were very divergent from this time, and in low tones they answered in their own tongue. Some of the soldiers made slighting remarks, but there are those among educated whites who have no serious moments, no serious thoughts; they have not time to be serious, and no inclination; but this was a serious time for those poor creatures; they knew the hour had arrived when they must say good-bye forever on earth to their red-skinned partners in life's joys and sorrows. No hand shake; no embrace; no crying; but a sorrowful, affectionate look, and they turn their back on them forever.

The women and children are taken down to Fort Snelling, and in a camp prepared for them they are put for the winter, and a strong guard placed about them to prevent any outrages being committed. The night the news was carried to them of the execution the wails of the poor creatures could be heard for a long distance away: "Rachael mourning for her children and would not be comforted, because they were not."

Much sorrow was expressed for them because we could but feel that they were unfortunate creatures, endowed with all the attributes of human beings.

The mortality among them was very great and hundreds died before the winter of suspense had passed away.

In April, 1863, the camp was broken up and the remaining ones were placed in a steamer for St. Louis, from whence they were to be sent up the Missouri River to the Crow Creek agency. Some died on the way, and as they left their homes and looked for the last time on their native hills, a dark cloud was crushing out their hearts. Soon after landing at Crow Creek every tepee had its sick and anxious hearts—mothers and children far away from their dead.

The deported ones joined their families in time, and as the years glide on they have had time for reflection, and the events, as they undoubtedly come trooping back to them, furnish food for thought.

CHAPTER XXVIII.

CAPTURE AND RELEASE OF JOE BROWN'S INDIAN FAMILY.

We knew Major Brown well. He was known to nearly all early settlers, because he came to Minnesota when the white people were very few. He felt that it was not well for man to live alone, a white man especially, and so he took unto himself a dusky bride. He was in government employ and a big white chief among his new found wife's people and to whom he was a friend.

As he grew in years his family grew also, and the dusky mother's household cares increased. Yes, they lived in a fine stone house, elegantly furnished, down on the Yellow Medicine below the agency, but which came in the way of his red brother's vengeance, and it was destroyed. The Brown family lived happily in their rather modern home. The Major attended to his official duties, and the wife and boys cultivated the land; but in common with all the others during these sad days, their only safety was in flight. Their home, including books and furniture, was totally destroyed. The father was a fugitive and his family prisoners. They did not suffer as some others did, because the wife and mother was a full blood, and was related to the

Sisseton tribe and had powerful friends among them. Their capture, captivity, and final release, as related by Samuel Brown, the fifteen-year-old boy, is an interesting recital. He says:

On Monday, the 18th day of August, I went to Yellow Medicine with my sister Ellen upon an errand. We met on the way an Indian named Little Dog, who told us that the Indians had killed a family at Beaver Creek, and were going to kill the whites as far as St. Paul, and that we must not tell any one about it, or they would kill us. He said he warned us at the risk of his own life. This was about noon. Soon after our arrival at Yellow Medicine an old squaw told us that we had better be getting away, as there would be trouble. We asked many of the other Indians about it, but they said they had heard of nothing of the kind. Another squaw afterward told us that she thought it must be the Yanktonais who were coming down to take the agency. We left them about half-past three o'clock. George Gleason had just left with Mrs. Wakefield and her children for below. When we reached home we told mother what we heard. She was very much scared and did not sleep any that night. About four o'clock next morning I heard some one outside calling in a loud voice a number of times for my mother, and then I heard Charles Blair, my brother-in-law (a white man), ask what was the matter, and the man, who was a half-breed named Royer, said that four hundred Yanktonais had arrived at the upper agency and were killing everybody. We then became very much alarmed, and had our oxen yoked at once to the wagon, put everything in we could, and started for Fort Ridgely. We had all the neighbors warned, and they went with us. They had three wagons, with ox teams. Four or five white men overtook us on the road, among them Garvey's cook (Garvey was the trader wounded at the agency, and who afterward died at Hutchinson.)

When we had gone about five miles we saw some men two miles ahead, near the bank of the river, but supposed they were farmers. The Yanktonais, whom we were afraid of, lived above us. We thought nothing about the men until we saw an Indian on a hill ahead of us. He beckoned to others, and before we knew it we were surrounded. De-wa-nea, of Crow's band, and Cut-Nose and Shakopee, three of the worst among the Lower Indians, came to us first. We were in the head wagon. Mother told them who we were, and they said we must follow them, and that we were all as good as dead. De-wa-nea said that the whites had taken him prisoner a good many times and that it was now his turn. He wanted the rest of the Indians to kill us all. There was an Indian in the party, John Moore's brother-in-law, who took our part, and he and his friends saved us from the others. This Indian had once come to our house when he was freezing and my mother took him in and warmed him. He told the other Indians that he remembered this, and that we should live. They insisted that my brother Angus should shoot one of the white men, but he refused to do so. Each of the Indians had one of the whites picked out to shoot as they came up. My mother said they were poor men and it would do no good to kill them. John Moore's brother-in-law said they should live if she wanted them to. The Indians made a great fuss about it, and said she ought to be satisfied with what she had got, but afterwards consented and told the men to start off. The women stayed with us. After the men had got off a little, Leopold Wohler, who had a lime-kiln at the agency, came back to the wagon after his boots, and an Indian told him if he didn't go away he would kill him. He started off with one boot, and came back again for the other, and the Indian drove him away again with the same threat. He went a short distance and came back again to kiss his wife. The Indians then became very much enraged, and acted so fiercely that he was glad to escape without further difficulty. There were ten Indians close to us, and twenty-five or thirty near, running into the houses. They made Angus and Charles Blair, who were riding horses, give them up. De-wa-nea put on my sister's bonnet and began singing a war song. He was very merry. He said the Indians were now going to have a good time, and if they got killed it was all right; that the whites wanted to kill them off, and were delaying the payment in order to do it by starvation, and that he preferred to be shot. We saw three men and a woman on the road terribly hacked up. This party had committed the murders. The men had been mowing together; their scythes and pitchforks were lying near by. Cut-nose showed us his thumb, from which a piece had been bitten near the nail, and he said it was done by one of these men while he was working the knife around in his breast; that he was very hard to kill, and he thought he would never die.

Cut-nose afterward went to a wagon and told a Scotch girl who was in it that he wanted her for his wife, and to get out and follow him. She refused, and he then drew his knife and flourished it over her, and she got out and went away with him. That was the last I saw of him until we got to camp. He was called Cut-nose because one of his nostrils had been bitten out. This was done by Other Day in a quarrel.

When we reached the camp of the Red Creek Indians, four miles above the Redwood River, they told us that the Agency Indians had sent word for all to come down there, and that those who did not come would be taken care of by the "Soldiers' Lodge." They were then about starting, and an Indian made Augus and myself hitch up a mule team which he said he had taken from Captain Marsh's men the day before. He said they had just heard a cannon at the fort and they wanted to go down and whip the whites there. This was about noon. We then went down to John Moore's house (this was where Other Day's horse was stolen), and they put us upstairs, where they had two or three women captives. We were there about an hour, when three Indians told us to come up to their camp on the hill, where we were to stop with John Moore's mother, or grandmother. We followed them, and when we got half-way up suddenly missed them. We supposed they hid from us, and we wandered on. We met a German woman who had seven or eight children with her, all under eight years of age,—two on her back, one under each arm and two following behind. They came along with us. We went to Moore's relative, but she said she knew nothing about us and couldn't take us, and that we had better go down to Crow's Village. We started, not knowing where to go, when a squaw, who was crying about the troubles, met us, and took us home with her. The Indians sent our team back to camp. They gave Augus and I blankets and moccasins, and we put them on and went down to see Little Crow. He told us to bring our folks down there, and no one should hurt us. This was Tuesday evening, about seven o'clock. He was in his own house, and the camp was pitched around it. We went back and brought our folks down. Little Crow put us up in the top room of the house, and gave us buffalo robes and everything to make us comfortable. He brought us a candle as soon as it was dark; he was very kind to us; he said he would take as good care of us as he could, but he didn't believe he could keep Charley Blair alive until morning. He gave him a breech clout and leggings, which he put on.

During the night an Indian or a half-breed came in the room downstairs where Crow was, and told him that we ought to be killed. We overheard what they said. The man was very ugly, and said no prisoners ought to be taken, and that we were related to the Sissetons, and had no claim on the Lower Indians, and there was no reason why we should be spared. He said he wanted Crow to call a council about it immediately. Crow told him that he saved us because we were his friends, and that he would protect us; that it was too late to hold a council that night, and he compelled him to leave.

He gave us plenty to eat, and came up several times during the night to see how we were getting along. We begged him to let Charley Blair go. He said he couldn't; that the Indians knew he was there, and would kill him (Crow) if he allowed it. We coaxed him for a couple of hours, when he consented, and brought an Indian, who took Charley down to the river and left him in the brush. He made his escape from there to the fort. Crow told us not to say anything about it, for the Indians would kill him, and that he did it because he had known our folks so long. He said the young men started the massacre, and he could not stop them. A week after that Akipu, an Upper Indian, came down from the Yellow Medicine Agency and took us up with him. From that time until our deliverance we remained with our relatives, and were well treated by them."

The foregoing recital is just as the boy gave it, and in subsequent conversations with the father it was substantially verified.

Major Brown, after recovering his family, lived for a few years, and did much toward assisting the Government in adjusting the many claims brought against it by persons who had suffered so much at the hands of the Indians. He died a number of years ago, but the members of his family live and are much respected in the community in which they live.

CHAPTER XXIX.

GOVERNOR RAMSEY AND HOLE-IN-THE-DAY.

Alexander Ramsey, of Minnesota, is the last of the famous coterie of war governors; a band that will be immortal. Curtin, of Pennsylvania; Dix, of New York; Dennison, of Ohio; Morton, of Indiana; Randall, of Wisconsin; Yates, of Illinois; Blair, of Michigan; Andrew, of Massachusetts; and Kirkwood, of Iowa;—a notable group, stalwart, rugged patriots with hearts beating as one. Comprehending the danger that menaced the nation, confronted with no easy task, these grand old stalwarts pledged their states to uphold, with men and money, the general government. They have passed away honored by a grateful country and beloved by the men who responded to their call. Governor Ramsey alone remains, and in the National Grand Army encampment held in St. Paul in 1896 he was a central figure. Passed, as he has, beyond the allotted time of man, measure full and running over, he saw the salvation of his country, proud of the part Minnesota's sons took in its restoration, and proud to meet them after the smoke of battle had cleared away. Governor Ramsey, being in Washington at the time of the first call for troops, promptly responded in person to the President, and tendered a regiment from Minnesota, and it was accepted; and it was the first to be accepted. He immediately telegraphed to Adjutant General William Henry Acker to at once issue

HOLE-IN-THE-DAY.

a call for one regiment of three months men.

The companies were soon filled up, and Adjutant-General Acker was commissioned as captain of Company "C." He was afterwards commissioned as captain in the Sixteenth U. S. Infantry, and was killed at Shiloh.

Governor Ramsey was elected United States Senator from Minnesota, and served his state faithfully and well, and was at one time Secretary of War. At this writing he is hale and hearty, honored by men of all political faith.

Governor Ramsey's part in the Indian trouble was more than commissioning officers and sending men to the frontier.

The Chippewas were in a turbulent state of mind, and Hole-in-the-Day, their chief, did not seem inclined to soften their feelings to the Government, but rather encouraged them in their desire to break their compact. He said to his people that "we had all we could manage, with our brethren in the South, and if they pleased to combine with the Sioux, their power could not be resisted."

This surely was cause for alarm,—alarm for the safety of the state, and it required strong measures to curb this uprising among these Indians. Commissioner Dole lost hope of successfully meeting the demands of the Indians, and dispatched a messenger to Governor Ramsey asking him to hasten to his relief. The Governor lost no time, and with two or three others were soon on the way. He did not go with an army carrying banners, but quietly and unostentatiously met the Chippeway chiefs, and soon adjusted all difficulties.

When it became known to Hole-in-the-Day that General Sibley had an overwhelming force, he was then desirous to befriend the state and assist in making a treaty of perpetual friendship with the whites, and assist them in fighting Little Crow. And after the battle of Wood Lake the

Winnebagoes, who were inclined to go to war against the "pale faces," concluded it best to court his favor and proclaim war against the Sioux. Prior to this, all the tribes in Wisconsin had sent their "wampums" to the Winnebago chief, and a council of war had been fixed for the 28th of September. There seemed to be indications that an unfriendly white element was stirring up strife among all our Indian neighbors, and hence the impression that it was emissaries from the South who were doing it. It came from high authority that evidence existed to show that "the Western tribes are going to join the South." It was a critical moment for this country. Slavery existed yet, and God's hand was laying heavily upon us. Federal reverses and Confederate successes cast a gloom over the North, and loyal men trembled, while the copper-head came forth and, with an exultant hiss, impeded the progress of the Government in its efforts to bring about an honorable peace. Under these depressing conditions Governor Ramsey, to whom all looked with so much solicitude, nerved himself to bring about an amicable settlement with the Chippewas.

In three days from the time of departure, Governor Ramsey returned, having effected a settlement of all misunderstandings on September 15th, 1862.

The public mind was relieved, for nearly every chief of the Nation being present to sign this treaty of peace, all hostile demonstrations ceased, and they evinced their further friendship by coming to St. Paul to return Governor Ramsey's visit, and tender their services to General Pope to operate against the Sioux.

The Governor assured them he was pleased to know they had not stained their hands in innocent blood, as the Sioux had done;—that he would communicate their desire to join the white soldiers to the big chief, General Pope, and he would send for them. The talk they had with the Governor so pleased them that they became confidential and talkative. Their responses thus far had been grunts and "ho, hos," but Chief Berry Hunter said the words they listened to "went right into his ears, and they were good," and although he was an old man he had not lost his reason. That they had come down to show their white brothers they felt very friendly, and never desired to have any other feeling towards them.

Big Dog, another of their noted chiefs, whose hands were very red, said he had painted them purposely, so that if he should kill an enemy and blood got on his hands it would not stain them.

Governor Ramsey extended them an invitation to ride in the "fire wagon" to St. Anthony (now East Minneapolis).

This meant that he would take them on the train. Railroading in Minnesota at this time was new to the white people, and the beautiful engines were objects of delight and admiration to them, and more so to the Indians, who were much interested in everything they saw in and about the locomotive, and they expressed great wonder at the steam whistle, and invariably ducked their heads as its shrill notes broke upon their ears. They did not wish to appear as cowards, but, like white soldiers dodging bullets after they had passed, so they inadvertently would "duck" when the whistle blew, and afterward have a hearty laugh over it.

CHAPTER XXX.

CHASKA—GEORGE SPENCER—CHASKA'S DEATH—THE "MOSCOW" EXPEDITION.

Chaska and George Spencer were great friends, and there was reason for it, as you will see. It was in George Spencer's store where the first shot was fired, and he was the victim. He ran upstairs, but the Indians surrounded the place and threatened to burn the store, which they probably would have done but for the fact they wanted the goods. They could not muster courage to go upstairs to kill him, because they naturally thought: "What would he be doing while we are trying to kill him?"

An old squaw got him out the back way and secreted him in her tepee, and the Indians finally burnt the building, and supposed he had perished in the flames. The squaw turned him over to his Indian friend Chaska, and when the other Indians, who supposed he was dead already, saw him quite alive, they were much puzzled, for they had no inkling of his escape.

He was the only white man at the agency who did escape, and can attribute it to the friendly ministration of those two native Americans, Chaska and the squaw. It was no miraculous escape, but a plain case of genuine friendship toward a white man by an Indian. An Indian

HOUSE OF CHASKA, A CIVILIZED IND....

will avenge a wrong—that is his nature. It is born in him, and it cannot be blotted out; so, too, will he remember a kindness with an equal degree of fidelity, and, under any and all circumstances, will "stick closer than a brother." Friend Spencer in this case found that the investment he had made in kindness to this red man was a paying one— it came in good time—his life was surely in jeopardy, and no miracle, but a faithful Indian, saved him, and this Indian was Chaska, a chief whom Little Crow had depended upon to help carry on the war. His friendship for Spencer was great, and when his friend's life was threatened, he with a double shooter in his hands would cry out: "Shoot if you like, kill him if you will, but two of you will come out of your saddles if you do."

Chaska dressed his friend in Indian garb and painted his face. It became necessary to kite him about, first in one friendly tepee and then in another, so that the spies could not keep track of him. I remember well the day I spoke with him. He had been wounded and was suffering from this, and the long days and nights of anxiety had told on him, but now that he could throw all this off he said he would soon be on the speedy round to complete recovery. Chaska was faithful to his friend of former years. He was desirous of becoming a white man so far as he could, by adopting their manners and customs. He came to see General Sibley one morning in his Indian garb, and the General said to him: "I am not pleased to see you in your blanket."

"Then I will wear it no more," was his reply. He washed off the paint from his face, trimmed his hair, and dressed as a citizen. He desired to live in a house rather than a tepee and to have his children attend school. This was the wish of all the friendly Indians. They instituted reforms in the social fabric, and in marrying, the rite was performed by an ordained minister, the same as among their white brethren. Poor Chaska, I remember well the night he died, for at the time a strong suspicion pointed toward a member of my own regiment, who was a clerk in the hospital department, and their never was a doubt but Chaska's death was by poison administered by this man. George Spencer, his white friend, said of him: "On the second day of our return from the Missouri, we rode along talking pleasantly of the future, he telling me how he would like to be situated on a small farm of land near me, and congratulating himself that his trouble was over, and that he would soon be restored to the bosom of his family. Alas, for my friend! He now sleeps tranquilly near the turbid waters of the Missouri, under the shadow of our intrenchments. Savage though he was, he was a noble man!"

The night he died he had gone around to his white friend's tent, where he was always welcome, and supped with him and arranged for carrying in the commissary wagon, a pack of furs he had captured. He went to his quarters after taking a dose of medicine and was soon taken ill. He sent for his white comrade, who went immediately to his bedside, to find him senseless, dying. In his delirium he predicted a thunderstorm that would shake the earth and blind the people the day he was put in the ground, and the prediction came true. He did not once recognize his friend, who remained with him, closing his eyes with a sorrowful heart. He died at the age of thirty-two, leaving a wife and two interesting children. He was faithful among the faithless.

THE SENTINEL.

CHAPTER XXXI.

THE "MOSCOW" EXPEDITION.

This expedition, well named "Moscow," will be remembered by the participants so long as they live. The government had decided to remove all the Indians to Fort Thompson, a military post on the Missouri, and after it had been done, it was found a little later that they were in a starving condition. General Pope communicated this fact to the authorities at Washington, and that the Indian agent had applied to him to furnish an escort for a supply train, that would be sent from Minnesota rather than from Sioux City, Iowa. Three companies were designated to undertake this perilous journey, and placed in command of Captain J. C. Whitney, of the Sixth Minnesota. It was impossible to hire teamsters to go, so an offer of twenty-five cents per day was made to the soldiers in addition to their $13 per month; but the undertaking was too hazardous and the offer was refused. The bid was raised until it reached $1.25 per day extra, when a few soldiers agreed to accept. On the 6th day of November a partial start was made, but one delay after another occurred until the case became desperate, and the teamsters finally got two dollars a day extra.

The fact was, the soldiers rebelled, and in order to frustrate the plans of the contractors the wagons were so disabled that it was impossible to move. Colonel Crooks, of the Sixth Minnesota, took matters in hand so vigorously that the soldiers knew that the expedition would have to move at all hazards, and it was foolish and dangerous to object and waste any more time. Several arrests of mutinous soldiers were made, but upon promises of better conduct they were released, and the "Moscow" expedition was finally and fully launched on the 20th day of November, 1863. The undertaking was hazardous, but the men were supplied with the best of Sibley tents and blankets in plenty. Under the most favorable circumstances it was not a picnic, but barring the stinging cold days and colder nights, with a few frozen noses, no serious mishap overtook the brave soldier boys of this celebrated "Moscow" expedition.

The return march was by way of Sioux City, Iowa, and the first post in Minnesota was reached on December 29th, 1863. During the trip the command encountered severe storms and the thermometer at times fell to 40 degrees below zero—but thirteen dollars a month in depreciated currency was a fair compensation.

Designed by A. P. Connolly.

CAMP POPE,
Where the troops assembled for the campaign of 1863.

CHAPTER XXXII.

CAMPAIGN OF 1863—CAMP POPE.

In October, 1862, General John Pope had informed General Halleck that five Minnesota regiments could be sent south by November 1, but local influences were at work to prevent the transfer of troops, as it seemed very likely that hostilities would be renewed by the Indians again in the spring, and the demand that the State should be fully protected against these roving bands was acceded to, and orders were forthwith issued to the various companies to proceed at once to points designated on the frontier and go into winter quarters. Rumors were afloat at all times, but there really was no danger, and the soldiers had little to do but attend to a light guard duty and while away the tedious hours as best they could. The campaign of 1863 was planned by General John Pope, and General H. H. Sibley, who was in command of the district of Minnesota, with headquarters at St. Paul, was selected to command the Minnesota column, and General Alfred Sully to command the column that was to proceed up the west bank of the Missouri.

These two columns were to co-operate for the final extinction of the Indians; but the low water of the Missouri prevented the plan from being carried out.

The rendezvous of the Sibley column was at a point near the mouth of the Red Wood River, and twenty-five miles above Fort Ridgely. The forces comprising the expedition organizing at this point were the Sixth, the Seventh and the Tenth Regiments of Minnesota Infantry, under Colonels William Crooks, William R. Marshall and James H. Baker; eight pieces of artillery, under command of Captain John Jones; the Mounted Rangers, under Colonel McPhail; Indian scouts and other small detachments, which brought the force up to 3,052 infantry, 800 cavalry and 146 artillerymen.

The camp, named in honor of General John Pope, then in command of the Department of the Northwest, was situated at the mouth of Red Wood River, in the vicinity of the place where the outbreak was inaugurated. The various regiments, composed of infantry, cavalry and artillery, rendezvoused here. Colonel William Crooks, of the Sixth Minnesota, was in temporary command, and soon after the troops began to assemble, guard mount, company and regimental drills were the order of the day.

The land upon which we were encamped was a perfect level, and in order to attain better discipline, and instruct the men in works of defense, a complete system of sod breastworks and bastions were erected about the camp, of sufficient width to admit of the sentinels being placed on the top of them. It was really a magnificent piece of engineering and reflected credit on the officer in command. The sentinels were instructed to "walk the beat" all in the same direction, turn about at the same time and retrace their steps, so that an enemy could not creep in between them. This was done to instruct the men in guard duty and keep them out of mischief, for there really was no danger.

On the 9th day of June, 1863, the monotony of the camp was relieved by the arrival of General Sibley and his staff. This official family consisted of Captain R. C. Olin, A. A. G.; Captain Forbes, brigade commissary; Captain Atchinson, ordnance officer; Captain Edward L. Corning, brigade commissary; Captain Kimball, A. Q. M.; First Lieutenants Douglas Pope, F. J. H. Beaver, Joseph R. Putnam and Charles H. Flandreau, aides-de-camp, and Rev. S. R. Riggs, brigade chaplain.

The cannon, placed across the river on the high bluff, boomed forth the intelligence that the cavalcade of brilliantly uniformed officers was approaching, and the General doffed his hat in salute as he rode down the long line of soldiers who stood at "present arms." General Henry H. Sibley, who had gained the confidence and universal respect and love of the soldiers, was again with us.

Soon after his arrival he received the sad intelligence of a beloved daughter's death. But the responsibilities resting upon him would not admit of days of mourning; there was no time for communion with grief; the needs of the hour reminded him of his duty.

While lying at Camp Pope, General Sibley heard that a party of Indians were on their way down to the settlements, and would cross Red Wood River at a certain point the next night. He at once gave orders that my own company, the one that had sustained such losses at Birch Coolie, should proceed at once to watch for and intercept this band. We received the orders at midnight, and with three days' rations, and sixty rounds of ammunition, started out on our mission in charge of First Lieutenant Harry J. Gillhams. We had no doctor with us; no team; not even an ambulance. I never thought our General knew of this, for he was a very careful man, and the question with me was: "If we are attacked and meet with losses in killed or wounded what shall we do with them in the absence of any means of transportation?"

We arrived at the point designated the next day about noon and halted. There was no going into camp, for we had no tents. We simply halted and waited for night and Indians. I was in hopes that the Indians would not come, and I got my wish. There were others hoping they would come, and among those most desirous for them to make their appearance were our three full blooded Indian soldiers we had captured, and who were present at the various battles the year before. One of them, Joe Alord, a powerful fellow, claimed to have a grudge against his own people. He said they had always treated him badly, and he wanted to fight them, but I was a little suspicious of him—did not think him sincere. This Alord formed a strong attachment for me, which endured until he was finally mustered out. He went south with us and stood the climate, and proved himself a faithful soldier. I at one time saved him from death by his own hands. He had been punished by the Colonel for an offense of which he said he was not guilty. I think myself he had been imposed upon, like "Old Dog Tray," by getting into bad company. The Colonel, as a punishment, ordered him to parade up and down the square with a bag of sand on his back. This was galling to the Indian, and calling me to one side, he said: "Sergeant, me kill me mine self; me kill me mine self!"

I tried to persuade him from his purpose, but he seemed

determined to carry out his threat, and I watched him closely. I could see he was very much aggrieved, for to him the humiliation was galling.

He grabbed a bayonet, and putting it to his breast, attempted to throw the weight of his body and thus push it through him. I jumped and kicked it from under him just in time and then put him in a cell until he became more reconciled. Soon after the close of the war he enlisted in the regular cavalry, but one morning he was missing. He had deserted, taking his horse and all his equipments with him; and although he was posted as a deserter, he was not heard of for many months.

When heard from it was to the effect that he had gone back to the Indians, taking the horse and all plunder with him. The old grudge against him was rekindled and intensified on account of the course he pursued against his people during the Sioux war, and some of the young bucks, engaging him in a controversy, it resulted in his death.

The Indian soldier Miller was inclined to be pious. He served until the close of the war, and afterwards was caught on the prairie in a severe thunder storm, from which he took refuge in a barn, which was struck by lightning and he was killed. The third was named Walker. At the outbreak he was home on vacation from Bishop Whipple's school at Faribault, Minn., and was taken prisoner. I have referred to these Indian soldiers once before. Walker was quite well educated and now lives near St. Paul.

These three Indian boys were with us on this midnight expedition, and I felt they would bear watching, because I could not make up my mind to the fact that they should want to so suddenly turn against their own people. About midnight the second night an incident happened that gave us some alarm for a little while. We were all on duty watching and listening for Indians. You have heard about the burnt child dreading the fire. Well, we had been seriously burnt at Birch Coolie, and did not relish another taste of the same sort of fire, and it is not astonishing under such circumstances how many Indian sounds there are to the square foot. Every minute some of us heard an Indian sound, and all at once Joe Alord skipped out in the darkness, and immediately he was followed by Miller. I at once thought it was treachery, and the same opinion prevailed among nearly all the boys. I was but a sergeant then and of course could not assume supreme authority. If I had been in command I should have held the remaining one as a hostage. He wanted to go after the other two and gained the consent of the lieutenant to do so, and away he went out in the darkness. I expected soon to hear the crack of the rifle, for I felt satisfied that they had proved false to us. After they were gone half an hour and returned to our lines with the news that the noise they heard was not Indians we all felt relieved.

. But the half hour was an anxious one, and we were rejoiced to have them return. The Indians we were sent out to intercept did not appear, and the next day our little expedition returned to camp.

CHAPTER XXXIII.

"FORWARD MARCH."

On the 16th day of June, 1863, with the thermometer 100 degrees in the shade, all things being in readiness, the column took up the line of march into the almost unexplored region of Dakota Territory.

This invading army was composed of nearly five thousand men, with a pontoon train, and an adequate ammunition and commissary train composed of 225 four and six-mule teams; and these, with the troops, really made a formidable army. The big train, five miles long, was necessary, because the expedition was headed for an unknown and hostile country, and expected to traverse a territory totally devoid of vegetables of any sort, and game would probably be very scarce.

The force was well organized, and the appearance of the train alone would awe the whole Sioux nation. It was a season of drouth such as was never before known in the West. The prairies were literally parched up with the heat, the grass was burned up, and the sloughs and little streams were dry. The fierce prairie winds were like the hot siroccos of the desert, and great clouds of dust, raised by the immense column, could be seen for miles and were viewed in wonder. We suffered from the heat, the dust and the weight of our knapsacks, gun and equipments, for the first day. The second day was as hot and dry, but the knapsacks were much lighter. Any one, even at this late date and so far removed from the days of the war, who thinks that a soldier's life is an easy one, that war is a picnic, is not endowed with common "horse sense." And yet there are those who thus express themselves.

The trains were soon being relieved of a part of their load by us drawing rations, and we had transportation to carry our individual loads.

I cannot in the few pages allotted me follow the daily march of General Sibley and his hosts; but will, after a hard day's march of eighteen prairie miles (twenty-five in God's country), with heavy knapsacks, halt, stack arms, pitch our tents and direct letters from

CAMP SIBLEY,

for such it was named, in honor of our commander.

The General had decided to observe Sunday as a day of rest, deeming it necessary for the welfare of man and beast. There is no doubt but better service was rendered for so doing, and General Sibley was honored for this proper respect shown the Lord's day.

The several camps were named after the officers in the command, the senior officers taking precedence; first, the colonels, then lieutenant-colonels, etc., etc. Nothing of an unusual nature other than a prairie fire occurred until we reached camp Atchison, where the forces were divided, and this will be the subject of a future chapter.

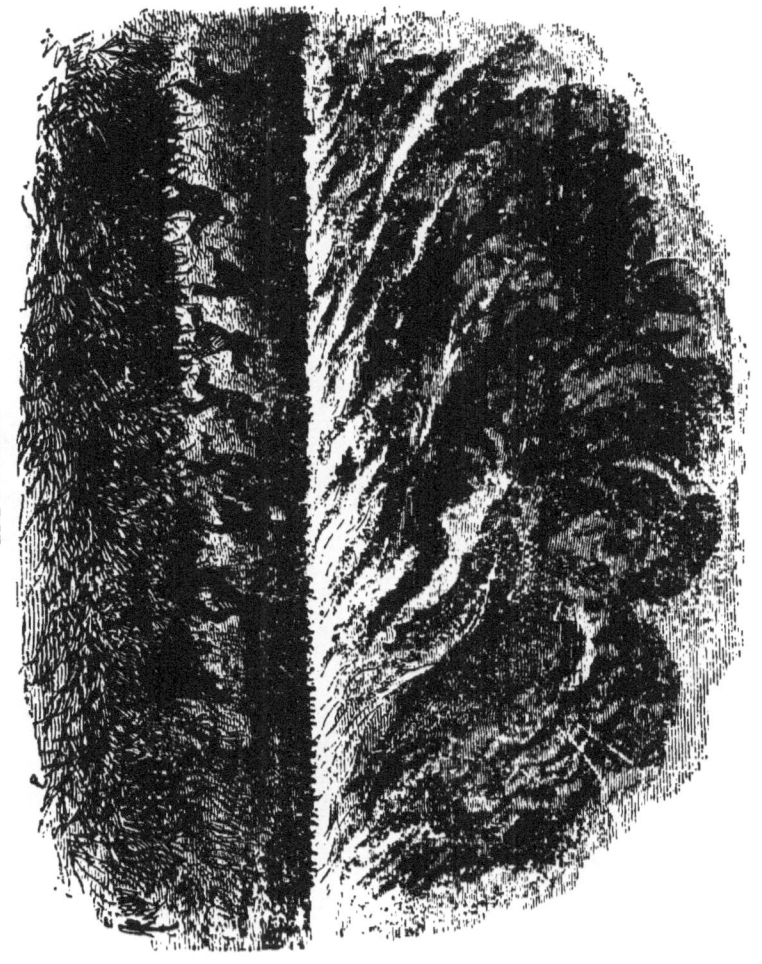

PRAIRIE ON FIRE.

CHAPTER XXXIV.

BURNING PRAIRIE—FIGHTING FIRE.

We started out on an exploring expedition to hunt Indians when we left Camp Pope. On the prairies there are enemies of various sorts—Indians, dust, heat and fire. The latter is a most formidable weapon with the Indian if the grass is plentiful and the weather dry, and they can use it to great advantage if the attacking party is not cool headed.

Our sentinels were always instructed to report fire at once, no matter how far off it might appear to be. This enemy came in good time—it appeared one night when there was a high wind.

The flames spread, becoming one vast sheet, sweeping over the prairies—a very roaring cataract of fire, the billows of which reached to the clouds. Coming on at this rapid, relentless rate, it would envelop and destroy the whole command.

To arms! to arms! we are called, by bugle and by drum, and in face of this enemy, at a "double quick," we march out to meet it. In case of fire the animals are frenzied, and it was a question at one time whether there would not be a stampede.

The only way to conquer this sort of an enemy is to

fight fire with fire, and this is done by burning away from you; so we started our fire, and as it burned away from us, we took possession of the burnt area as the fire demon in the rear came roaring on to consume us in his hot embrace. The red flames roared on high, the dense smoke obscured the moon and the stars, the atmosphere was stifling and thick with coal black dust, and the roar, as the fire fiend rolled on towards us, would have struck terror to the stoutest heart did we not know that his fury would soon be spent.

CHAPTER XXXV.

DEATH OF LITTLE CROW.

We will halt the column for a little and hunt in another direction for Little Crow. He had not been captured and would not surrender after the battle of Wood Lake in 1862. Carried away with the idea that he would receive proper recognition and the confidence of the Indians he started away towards the British dominions. Devil's Lake was always a favorite "summer resort" for the Indians, and perhaps we can find him there.

In the State of Dakota, nearly five hundred miles west from St. Paul, Minn., is the celebrated Minnewakan, or Devil's Lake. It is about sixty-five miles in length, and its waters are as salt as are those of the ocean. The immediate shores are part timber and part prairie; but a mile beyond, the country is one vast rolling prairie, destitute of trees, and dotted over with little lakes of salt water. This inland sea is a romantic place, and is well filled with fish, and game quite plentifully can be found there. Among other things are sea gulls and swan. The shore of the lake is covered with petrified wood, and the bones of fishes and animals are in abundance.

To this neighborhood Little Crow and his followers, after the defeat at Wood Lake, Minn., wended their way and encamped, where they were joined by nearly all the Minnesota Sioux who had not surrendered or been captured. There were in all about 4,000 souls, and among them were Yanktonais. During the winter the chief sent out runners with messages and presents to many of the Western tribes, and endeavored to enlist them as allies in a general war.

About the first of June Little Crow went to St. Joseph and Fort Garry to gain recognition from the British, as well as to obtain ammunition, but both were refused him.

When at St. Joseph Little Crow had on a black coat with velvet collar, a lady's fine shawl adorned his head, and another was knotted around his waist. He had discarded his rifle, and carried a pistol instead, which latter was one of his trophies from the last summer's raid. He had learned of the deportation of his friends to the Missouri, of which the white residents there had as yet received no information. Crow received the news in advance from an Indian who had outstripped the regular mail. He and sixty of his braves had a war dance, after which he made a speech, in which he said that he considered himself as good as dead, but that he still had plenty of warriors upon whom he could rely, and would not be caught during the summer. He failed to get the recognition he thought he was entitled to as commander-in-chief of the Sioux army then in the field. It is a little strange that he could not be recognized, when cannibal kings from the islands of the sea can get recognition, and the devotees of royalty will tumble over each other to pay their respects to a lecherous, murderous Turk.

Being disappointed in this, he made up his mind to slip through the cordon of posts that had been established for the protection of the people, and while General Sibley with his army was hunting for him away towards the Missouri, he would, single-handed and alone, go horse stealing down in the settlements.

Alas! How are the mighty fallen! From a commander-in-chief, seeking recognition of a foreign nation, he at once becomes a vagabond horse thief.

His son, Crow, Jr., was his only confidant, and to him he said:

"I am getting old and cannot fight the white men, but will go below, steal horses from them for you children, so you may be comfortable, and then I can go away where they cannot catch me."

The whole party that went with the fallen chief numbered sixteen men and one squaw.

Crow, Jr., whose Indian name was Wa-wi-nap-a (one who appeareth), was with his father near Hutchinson, Minn., picking berries to "stay their stomachs," when they were discovered by a Mr. Lamson and his son Chauncey. This was Friday evening, July 3, 1863, and the skirmish that followed between Crow, his son, and the Lamsons prevented the Sioux chief from celebrating the Fourth of July in any sort of patriotic manner, for two shots from the trusty rifle of Mr. Lamson sent Crow's soul on its eternal mission to the happy hunting ground of his fathers. Mr. Lamson and his son were out in the country and they saw two Indians picking berries in an "opening" in the woods. The Indians did not discover the white men, who were taking aim at them. Mr. Lamson had crept cautiously forward among the vines and rested his gun against a tree and fired. His first shot took effect, but not a deadly one, as evinced by the loud yell of his victim, who fell to the ground severely wounded.

With prudence and caution Mr. Lamson retreated a short distance, where he could obtain shelter from behind some bushes.

The wounded Indian, not to be foiled, crept after him, and thus they were brought face to face. Another shot from the white man and the Indian was dead. His companions, his own son and another Indian, mounted a horse and fled.

The Indian's shot, however, had not gone amiss, for it lodged in Mr. Lamson's shoulder, and he being some distance from his son, was supposed by him to be killed. The son returned to town to give the alarm. A quick response brought men to the scene of conflict, where they found the dead Indian, but Mr. Lamson was missing. A singular thing about it was that Crow was laid out, his head resting on his rolled-up coat, and he had a new pair of moccasins on. It would appear as though his son returned to make sure of his father's death, and finding him dead, he performed this last deed. *

Mr. Lamson's wound was a severe one, but he made his way back to his home, which he reached about two o'clock the next morning. Little Crow's body was brought to town, and the coat he had on was recognized as belonging to a man who had been found murdered some weeks before.

The body of this murderous old chief, after it lay in state

---

*Brown's Valley, Minn., Nov. 30.—Nathan Lamson, the man who, during the Indian outbreak in Minnesota in 1862, killed Little Crow, the famous Sioux chieftain, died to-day on his farm across the line in South Dakota, aged 96.—[Chicago Times-Herald, Dec. 1, 1896.

Designed by A. P. Connolly.
MR. LAMSON SHOOTING LITTLE CROW NEAR HUTCHINSON, MINN., IN AUGUST, 1863.

on the ground for a day or two, was dumped into an unhonored grave, and no tears of regret were shed for him. While this was being done down in Minnesota, a military train five miles long was in pursuit of him up in Dakota; and the news did not reach General Sibley for two weeks. The description given of this Indian was so accurate that the General said it was no other than Little Crow. This again was corroborated by his son, who was some weeks after captured in a starving condition.

Thus ended the ignominious life of Little Crow, the great Sioux chief who had influenced his people to believe that the time had come for them to reclaim their lost empire.

CHAPTER XXXVI.

LITTLE CROW, JR.—HIS CAPTURE.

After the death of Crow, senior, as narrated in the preceding chapter, his son and heir, Wo-wi-nap-a, becomes an important character in this chapter, and we will follow him and hear what he has to say about his father's death.

When he was satisfied that his father was dead he started off he knew not where. He was a fugitive, a miserable creature, bereft of home, country and parents—a human being without a country, but with a soul—in a land where every hand was raised against him; a fugitive from an enraged white people because of the sins of his father. He hid by day and traveled by night until beyond the white settlements. He was captured by a company of soldiers who were out hunting Indians in the region of Devil's Lake, Dakota. When captured he was in a starving condition and glad to get even among Uncle Sam's soldiers. He was questioned as to his father and where he had been. He said:

"I am the son of Little Crow; my name is Wo-wi-nap-a, and I am sixteen years old. Father said he was getting old and wanted me to go with him to carry his bundles. He left his wives and other children behind. There were sixteen men and one squaw in the party that went below with us. We had no horses, but walked all the way down to the settlements. Father and I were picking red berries near Scattered Lake at the time he was shot. It was near night. He was hit the first time in the side, just above the hip. His gun and mine were lying on the ground. He took up my gun and fired it first, and then fired his own. He was shot the second time while firing his own gun. The ball struck the stock of the gun and then hit him in the side near the shoulder. This was the shot that killed him. He told me that he was killed and asked me for water, which I gave him. He died immediately after. When I heard the first shot fired I laid down and the man did not see me before father was killed.

"A short time before father was killed an Indian named Hi-a-ka, who married the daughter of my father's second wife, came to him. He had a horse with him, also a gray-colored blanket that he had taken from a man whom he had killed, to the north of where father was killed. He gave the coat to my father, telling him that he would need it when it rained, as he had no coat with him. Hi-a-ka said he had a horse now and was going north. He further said that the Indians who went down with them had separated, and he had not seen them since."

After the death of his father Young Crow took both guns and started for Devil's Lake. He had no ammunition, but found a cartridge and cut it into slugs. With this he shot a wolf and ate some of it. His strength gave out, and twenty-six days after his father was killed he was captured.

The old chief was a great wooer of the fair sex, for his son said of him:

"My father had two wives before he took my mother;

the first one had one son, the second a son and daughter; the third wife was my mother. After taking my mother he put away the first two; he had seven children by my mother; six are dead; I am the only one living now; the fourth wife had four children born; do not know whether any died or not; two were boys, two were girls; the fifth wife had five children; three of them are dead, two are living; the sixth wife had three children; all of them are dead; the oldest was a boy, the other two were girls; the last four wives were sisters."

This young savage was cared for and finally sent away to the reservation. Having found the whereabouts of Little Crow and disposed of him, we will return to the command.

CHAPTER XXXVII.

CAMP ATCHISON—GEORGE A. BRACKETT'S ADVENTURE—LIEUTENANT FREEMAN'S DEATH.

Camp Atchison was the most important of all the camps on the whole route. It was here the General was visited by some three hundred Chippewa half-breeds, led by a Catholic priest named Father Andre, who told him that the Indians, hearing that General Sully, who was marching up the west side of the Missouri with a large body of troops, was delayed on account of low water, were deflecting their course in the hope of being reinforced by the Sioux inhabiting the country west of the Missouri.

The General, upon becoming satisfied of this, decided to push on as rapidly as possible after them, and to facilitate the movement he formed a permanent post at Camp Atchison, which is located about fifty miles southeast from Devil's Lake, where he left all the sick and brokendown men, and a large portion of his ponderous train, with a sufficient guard to protect them if attacked. With these arrangements completed, the column, with twenty-five days' rations for 1,500 infantry, 500 cavalry, 100 pioneers and artillery, started by forced marches to overtake the Indians before they reached the Missouri River.

On the morning of July 20th the General, with his selected men and reduced train, left Camp Atchison to pursue the Indians and engage them in battle. Attached to the expedition in the capacity of contractor was Mr. George A. Brackett, who met with an experience, the memory of which will remain with him during his life. It is most interesting and exciting, and his own version of it, as narrated at the "camp fire" when he found his old St. Anthony friends and Captain Chase's company, known as the "Pioneers," will be read with interest. Mr. Brackett says:

On the fourth day out, in company with Lieutenant Ambrose Freeman, of the Mounted Rangers, we left the main column for the purpose of adventure and game. I had my train started and in good hands, and got permission for the Lieutenant to accompany me. Five miles away, having met nothing worthy of note, we surveyed the country from the summit of a range of hills, when we saw several scouts not very far away. We struck a parallel course, believing we were moving in the same direction as the main column. While watering our horses in the lake, we espied two other scouts on the opposite side doing the same thing. We then moved farther on, over the range of bluffs, covering about three-quarters of a mile. We followed along parallel, or perhaps a little to the left of the main body, a distance of three miles. Lieutenant Freeman saw three antelopes, an old one and two young ones, in the distance. We fired and wounded the old one, who made off around the bluff. I held the Lieutenant's horse and he chased her on foot, which took us off our course some distance round the bluffs. We traversed a section of country bordering a large lake, near which we succeeded in killing the antelope.

As we were coming down to the lake and while the Lieutenant was creeping up toward the antelope, I again saw scouts on the opposite side of the lake, and the train was in sight on the hillside several miles distant. Instead of taking our course back, we had a curiosity to go around the lake to where we saw the scouts. On our way around we saw cherry bushes newly cut and piled up, and I set about to tear them down. Lieutenant Freeman persisted in saying that they were Indian signs and that Indians were in the vicinity. In preparation for them we cocked our rifles and made around the bushes, so as not to put ourselves in a too exposed position. We took our course, as we supposed, towards the train, or where the train had recently passed.

Between one and two o'clock we discovered three objects a long distance off, but between us and the train's course, and making for the train. This action, as soon as we came near enough to judge, convinced us that they were Indians, yet we kept on toward them, and they were making preparations to meet us, one leading and the other two riding their horses. We got all ready to give them a trial, they creeping around on one side of the bluff and we creeping around to meet them. I saw one with a straw hat on rise up and recognized him as one of our scouts. He beckoned us to come towards him. From all the description I had of him I supposed him to be Chaska, and the other two were full blood Sioux. Both had government horses, and armed, one with a Springfield and the other a carbine. I asked him where General Sibley was. They pointed to a hill, I should judge, three miles away from where we stood, in the direction where the train passed.

I saw a large number of men on a bluff, judged to be

about two hundred in number, whom I supposed to be General Sibley's men looking for us. We all started directly for them, and as we did so, saw what we supposed to be a guard of cavalry starting towards us. After we had started the scouts turned to a little lake to water their horses, but the Lieutenant and myself having previously watered ours, did not go with them. We still saw the cavalry, as we supposed, about fifteen in number, coming towards us.

I remarked to Lieutenant Freeman that they must have turned back, as they had disappeared and were out of sight. We were soon surprised, however, by seeing fifteen Indians charging upon us as with a flag of truce; but they were not coming evidently in a friendly spirit, as they fired a volley upon us. I yelled to the scouts that they were Indians, and remarked to Lieutenant Freeman that we had better at once join the scouts, which we endeavored to do. When we got within twenty or twenty-five rods of the scouts we were riding about three rods apart. One Indian rode up to Lieutenant Freeman and shot an arrow through his back, on the left side, and at the same time another Indian dismounted and discharged his gun at me, but I laid low on my horse's neck, as close as I possibly could, and he shot over me, and Chaska stepped up to the top of a knoll and shot this same Indian who had fired at me.

As Lieutenant Freeman dropped from his horse I asked him if he was hurt. He replied, "I am gone." He wished me to cut a piece of string which was around his neck, and supported a part of the antelope which he was carrying. As I cut the string he changed his position more on his side and more up hill. He asked faintly for water,

George A. Brackett Telling the Thrilling Story of His Escape to the Members of Capt. Chase's Company of "Pioneers."

THE MINNESOTA MASSACRE OF 1862.

Price, to any address, { 60 Cents in Paper.
$1.00 and $1.50 in Cloth.

A. P. CONNOLLY, Chicago.

which I gave him from my canteen, and by this time the scouts had mounted their horses and left us. The Indians were then all around us, and one at the side of the lake; but as the scouts ran toward them they fell back. Lieutenant Freeman, by this time being dead, I took his rifle and revolver and followed the scouts as fast as I could. The Indians mentioned as near the lake, seeing the Liuetenant's horse, which followed me, left us and started for the horse, thus enabling me to overtake the scouts. The Indians succeeded in catching the horse, and the whole crowd again started after us. We rode for about four miles, when we were overtaken and surrounded by them by the side of a little marsh. We all jumped from our horses. The scouts made motions and ran up to meet them, but Chaska motioned for me to jump into the tall rushes on the marsh. I saw nothing more of the scouts, and the Indians all rushed down to where the horses were. I cocked my rifle, and lay in the rushes within ten feet of where they were, and heard them quarrel about the possession of the horses. They presently settled their dispute and started off, for fear, as I supposed, of being overtaken by some of our forces. They took their course around the marsh in which I lay for an hour; this was about three p. m. A shower came up, and immediately after it cleared I started on my course, with the sun to my back, and traveled for two hours. I followed this direction for two days, stopping in marshes during the night. On the evening of the second day I struck a river of clear water, about a quarter of a mile wide, running in a southerly direction. Next morning I stated due south, and traveled until almost night, when I took a westerly course, concluding that the trail was not in that direction; traveled a little to north of west, and struck Gen. Sibley's trail the afternoon of the third day, about twelve miles from where we camped the night before. I left the main column, and made the deserted camp that night. I started next morning on the back track for Camp Atchison, and made the painful journey in two days, arriving there the second night, between eight and nine o'clock, making the distance of the four camps in two days, bareheaded, barefooted and coatless. I was obliged to leave my rifle on the last day of my travel, but I could not carry it any farther, and made up my mind that this would probably be my last day. It was probably about nine o'clock, and I was about to give up when I came to a few tents and found them to be those of the Pioneers (Captain Chase's company of the Ninth Minnesota Infantry), and fell to the ground faint and unable to rise again. But, thank God! around that fire were sitting some of my old St. Anthony friends, who kindly picked me up and carried me to my tent.

I lost my coat, hat and knife in the fight the first day, so I took Lieutenant Freeman's knife, and with it made moccasins of my boot legs, as my boots so chafed my feet in walking that I could not possibly wear them. These improvised moccasins were constantly getting out of repair, and my knife was much needed to keep them in order for use, as well as to make them in the first place. But just before reaching the trail of the expedition on the fifth day I lost the knife, and the loss, I felt at the time, would have decided my fate if I had much farther to go. But a kind Providence was in my favor, for almost the first object that greeted my eyes upon reaching the trail was a knife, old and worn to be sure, but priceless to me. This incident some may deem a mere accident, but let such a one be placed in my situation at that time and he would feel with me that it was given in answer to a prayer made to the great Giver of Good. On the third day, about ten miles from the river spoken of, I left Lieutenant Freeman's rifle on the prairie because I became too weak to carry it longer; besides, it had already been so damaged by rain that I could not use it. I wrote upon it that Lieutenant Freeman had been killed, and named the course I was then pursuing. The pistol I retained and brought with me to Camp Atchison.

While wandering I lived on cherries, roots, birds' eggs, young birds and frogs, caught by my hands, all my ammunition but one cartridge having been spoiled by the rain of the first day. That cartridge had a gutta percha case and was preserved. It was my only hope for fire when I should need it, or when I dared venture to make one. I had also some water-proof percussion caps in my portmanteau, which were also put to good use. I took one-half the powder in the cartridge, with a percussion cap, and with the use of my pistol and some dried grass, started a fire at which I cooked a young bird. How did I catch the bird? Well, Providence again favored me, and as I was lying low and making no noise, the bird wandered so near that by firing a stick I had with me in such a manner as to make it whirl horizontally, it struck the bird on the side of the head and broke its neck. This was on the second night. On the fourth I used the remainder of the cartridge in the same way and for a like purpose. The rest of the time I ate my foot uncooked. Except some hard bread (found at the fourth camp mentioned above), which had been fried and then thrown in the ashes. I have forgotten one sweet morsel (and all were sweet and very palatable to me), viz., some sinews spared by wolves from a buffalo carcass. As near as I am able to judge I traveled in the seven days at least two hundred miles. I had ample means for a like journey in civilized localities, but for the first time in my life found gold and silver coin not legal tender. My boot-leg moccasins saved me, for a walk of ten miles upon such a prairie, barefooted, would stop all farther progress of any person accustomed to wearing covering upon the feet. The exposure at night, caused more particularly by lying in low and wet places, in order to hide myself, was more prostrating to me than scarcity of food. The loneliness of the prairies would have been terrible in itself, but for the drove of wolves that after the first day hovered, in the day time, at a respectful distance, and at night howled closely around me, seemingly sure that my failing strength would soon render me an easy prey. But a merciful Providence has spared my life by what seems now, even to myself, almost a miracle.

The body of Lieutenant Freeman was afterwards found and buried by members of General Sibley's main force. An arrow had pierced his breast, and the tomahawk and scalping knife had left bloody traces about his head. He was buried on the desolate plain, five hundred miles away from his beloved, bereaved wife and children. After the war closed his body was exhumed, carried to his late home, and re-interred by loving hands, with all the honors due a brave soldier. The peculiar circumstances of his death, my last moments with him, my subsequent days of weary, dangerous wandering, my suffering, anxiety and happy deliverance have made an impression upon my memory so indelible that time has not, nor cannot efface them.

My friend Brackett and myself came to St. Anthony,

Minn., on the same day, May 1st, 1857, and we "put up" at the same hotel, and it is most interesting to hear him relate this wonderful adventure and marvelous escape. He yet lives to tell the story, and poor Freeman! It seemed sad to leave him in his lonely grave on the prairie wild, but such is the fate of war.

CHAPTER XXXVIII.

BATTLE OF BIG MOUND.

A few days after leaving Camp Atchison scouts began to report to General Sibley that Indians in large numbers were between us and the hills beyond. Everything indicated this, and the evidences were that we were soon to have a battle.

We came in sight of the Indians every day, but nothing decisive until July 24th, when we overtook them. Scouts reported a large body of Indians, with Red Plume and Standing Buffalo among them, encamped by the very lake near which the General intended camping. Standing Buffalo was not there as a hostile, and it was a surprise all around. The General, satisfying himself that a determined resistance would be offered us, corralled his train and made such disposition of the troops as he deemed necessary. It was here where Dr. Weiser, of the First Minnesota Rangers, was killed while parleying with a delegation from the hostile camp, and it was treachery, pure and simple. The battle was opened by Whipple's battery, and while the cannon boomed and sent leaden hail and death among the fleeing Indians, the artillery of Heaven opened amid a furious thunder storm, and a private of Colonel McPhail's command was killed.

BATTLE OF BIG MOUND, DAKOTA.

Designed by A. P. CONNOLLY.

Fought between General Sibley's forces and the Sioux, on July 24th, 1863. The Indians were defeated.

The Indians in this affair lost eighty-seven killed and wounded and a vast amount of property.

A portion of our command made forty-six miles that day. My own regiment was ordered in pursuit, and we followed them for ten miles, after having already marched eighteen. An order had been sent by an aide for the pursuing troops to bivouac where they were, but being misunderstood, instead of camping, as it was intended, we returned, having been on the march all night. As we came into camp we found that an early reveille had been sounded, and the troops were about ready to march. The part of the command that had joined in the pursuit and returned during the night was so completely exhausted that the whole force was compelled to rest for a day. This battle was a decided victory, counting heavily in the scale of advantage, as it put the savages on the run to a place of safety and materially disabled them from prosecuting further hostilities.

After the battle of the Big Mound, as narrated, the command was compelled to take one day's rest on account of the over-taxed condition of the troops. The next day we marched over the same ground, and it was a comical yet interesting sight to witness the wholesale abandonment of buffalo robes, camp equippage and "jerked" meat; robes by the thousands and meat by the tons had been thrown away by the Indians in their hurry to get out of harm's way. We found dogs that had been harnessed up and loaded down with cooking utensils, dead;—they had died from sheer exhaustion. The prairies as far as the eye could penetrate on either side presented this condition of abandonment by the Indians, of their property and winter's supply of food. As far as the eye could penetrate on either hand were evidences of their hasty flight, as if swept with the besom of God's wrath. The men would "right about" and fight the soldiers, and then turn, and running towards their fleeing families, urge them to still greater exertion to get away from the avenging army.

In the sand on the bank of the lake, I found a tiny pappoose moccasin, and could see the imprint and count each separate toe of the little foot in the sand, as it probably was dragged along by the anxious mother, who was too heavily laden to carry her little baby. I thought,—poor, helpless child, not in the least responsible for its unhappy condition, and yet made to suffer. So with all classes of God's humanity;—the innocent too often made to suffer, not only with the guilty, but for the guilty, and in our decisions we should be careful lest we injure innocent persons. The fresh made graves we found on this trail told their sorrowful story,—the little Indian spirit had taken its flight,—the body was buried and the heart-broken mother hurried on to keep up with her people, and get away from the army.

READY TO GO INTO ACTION.

CHAPTER XXXIX.

BATTLE OF DEAD BUFFALO LAKE.

After the decisive battle of the Big Mound the Indians made up their minds evidently that the army and destruction was in their rear, and their Rubicon must be reached and crossed or annihilation was their portion, hence activity was apparent among them. The great impediment to their active work in the field and hasty flight was their families, and it required good generalship to successfully manage this retreating host.

The next decisive engagement with them was fought on July 26th; known as the battle of "Dead Buffalo Lake," so designated from the fact that the carcass of a big buffalo was found on its shores.

This day strict orders had been given that there should be no shooting within the lines. This was made necessary from the fact of a soldier having been wounded the day before from the careless use of a rifle in the hands of a comrade. We were going along at an easy jog, when all at once a beautiful deer went bounding along. He seemed terribly frightened, and evidently had been surprised by the skirmishers ahead. All orders were forgotten, and a general stampede was made for this beautiful deer. Shots were fired after him, but he made his escape, and it did seem too bad, for we were hungry for deer meat. The general thought we had met the Indians again, and aides were sent to the front, with orders for the proper disposition of the troops. As the Indians were known to be in large numbers not far ahead, the General was pardoned for his surmises.

We passed their abandoned camp early in the morning, but about noon the scouts reported a large body of Indians coming down upon us from various directions. The command was placed in line of battle, and soon the skirmishers, in command of Colonel William Crooks, opened fire, supported by Lieutenant Whipple's six-pounder.

The savages came swooping down on us, and it seemed as though they sprang up out of the earth, so numerous were they.

There were those among them who knew something of the tactics of war, and they attempted a vigorous flank movement on the left of the column, which was promptly checked by Captain Taylor and his mounted Rangers. Another determined attack was made which was handsomely repulsed by two companies of the Sixth Minnesota, under Colonel Averill.

A running fire was kept up until about three o'clock, when a bold dash was made to stampede the animals which were herded on the bank of a lake.

This attempt was promptly met and defeated by Wilson's and Davy's cavalry and six companies of the Sixth Minnesota, under Major McLaren. The Indians, foiled at all points, and having suffered serious losses in killed and wounded, retired from the field, and galloped away after their families, who, a few miles ahead, were hurrying on towards the Missouri river. Our animals were so jaded they could not stand a forced march. The reason was very apparent. We had our regular rations, while the horses and mules were on short rations on account of the hot weather burning up the grass, and, besides, the alkali water was as bad for beast as for man.

We were obliged to dig wells every night for water before we could get our supper, for we could not use the water from the alkali lakes. As many as sixty wells were dug in a night. Think of it,—each company obliged to dig a well in order to get water for supper, but this was one of the daily duties of the soldier. It is astonishing how the "boys in blue" could adapt themselves to every condition and circumstance. I am on a tender spot now,—"the boys in blue." 'Tis true times are changed; a few of us are alive yet, and perhaps we are just a little bit "stuck on ourselves"; but, "the old soldier," as we are now dubbed, cannot forget "the boys in blue." In a few years more a new generation will have control of our government, but the wonderful years from 1861 to 1865 will not be forgotten. If we do not give our government, body and soul, into the hands of foreigners who cannot speak our language it is possible that the memory of the "boys in blue" will remain with us for a time yet. They were a mighty host then, and the tramp, tramp, tramp of their feet as they marched to defeat and victory will go down the centuries;—but, I must come back to my narrative.

CHAPTER XL.

BATTLE OF STONY LAKE—CAPTURE OF A TETON—
DEATH OF LIEUTENANT BEAVER.

On the morning of July 28th, just as the command was breaking camp at Stony Lake, we were attacked by Indians, in full force.

General Sibley had the expeditionary forces so well in hand that the enemy could not possibly do us any harm. We halted but a moment, as some of the scouts came riding furiously towards us, followed by Indians intent on their capture. The boys cheered as they came within our lines. The battery was ordered to the front, and soon threw a shell among the Indians, who then galloped around on the flank, while another squad came immediately upon our rear; but, the whole column, in a solid square, moved on. The engagement took place on the prairie, and it was a beautiful sight to see, the regularity with which the column moved. First, two companies of cavalry skirmishers, and at a proper interval two companies of infantry; the same order was preserved in the rear, and flankers on the right and left, so as to form a hollow square. In the center were the reserve troops, stores of all sorts, and the artillery.

The teams were so fixed as to make it impossible to get up a stampede. The Indians resort to their peculiar tactics to stampede the teams,—they tried it to its fullest extent on this occasion, but without avail. They did not impede our progress in the least, and as the column moved right along, they soon gave up the attempt, and we pressed them so closely they allowed the killed and wounded to fall into our hands. The casualties were light, because the shells that were thrown among them did but little damage.

The cavalry in this case was effective, and crowded the Indians, as they charged them with drawn sabre.

This was the last stand the Indians made in a body, and they hastened on towards the Missouri river, which they finally crossed at a point near where Bismarck, North Dakota, now stands. They made a determined resistance, and had been repulsed in three successive engagements, and their situation was critical in the extreme,—the victorious army in the rear and the Missouri in front.

After the Indians had given up the fight and had ridden ahead to urge their families on, and we had buried the dead and cared for the wounded, we pushed on after them.

A young Teton chief, who was out on a tour of observation, was captured by some of the cavalry, and the circumstances and manner in which it was done are interesting.

Thousands of us saw the strange object, but the men who captured him were the more interested observers, and the narrator says:

"As the scouts approached it, a dark, motionless object was seen lying upon the ground. Coming nearer, some one cried out: 'It's an old buffalo robe'; but, as one stooped to pick it up, it sprang from the earth and bounded off like a deer, arms extended, and flying swiftly, in a zig-zag man-

Designed by A. P. Connolly.

BATTLE OF STONY LAKE, DAKOTA, JULY 28TH, 1863.
Indians defeated and slaughtered in great numbers by General Sibley's troops.

ner. It was a broad mark for the carbines, but where in it was the motive power? It was impossible to tell. Some thirty shots were fired, all hitting the robe, but still he kept on with the same zig-zag motion, so that it was impossible to hit him.

"At last one of the guides reined up near him and, placing a revolver to his head, fired, but he dodged and escaped the ball.

"He now stopped, dropped the robe, and threw up both hands, in token of surrender."

The robe he wore was literally riddled with bullets, but not a scratch upon the body of the Indian. His gallantry and his lordly bearing won the admiration of his captors, and placing him behind one of the scouts they bore him away in triumph, and presented him to General Sibley, to whom he extended his hand in friendly salute, but which was declined until he had made his statement, and assured the General that his hands were not stained with innocent blood. Being thus convinced, General Sibley shook him by the hand, and they became friends. He belonged to the Teton band, which is one of the largest divisions of the Dakota Nation. They lived west of the Missouri, and his information was that they were interested observers, but had no sympathy with, nor taking no part in, the war.

He and his father, who was one of the head chiefs, were out on a visit to the Yanktonians, and, learning that they were soon to have a fight with the soldiers, his curiosity prompted him to go as an observer. His curiosity was satisfied, and he retired with the balance, but had stopped in a clump of grass to allow his pony to graze. While here he had fallen asleep, and the pony was the object that first attracted the attention of the scouts, which resulted in the Indian's capture, as above narrated.

He was a prisoner with us for five days, during which time he was treated with some consideration as the heir apparent to the chieftainship of his tribe. He was about twenty years old; a fine looking fellow, tall and athletic. He became strongly attached to the General and the staff.

General Sibley afterwards learned of this Indian's death. He had given the boy, on his departure, a letter to his father, commending him for refusing to take up the tomahawk against the whites, and in appreciation of this, that he had kept the son for a few days in his camp and then gave him his liberty, so that he might return to his own people. It was good policy, because the letter, being found in his possession, indicated to the Indians that General Sibley was not responsible for his death.

A few days after his departure, a party of miners, who had been up in Idaho, were coming down the Missouri river, and at the very place where our men had reached the river and filled their canteens the Indians were lying in wait for the descending miners.

The young Teton desired peace, and rushed toward them waving General Sibley's letter over his head. They, not understanding his signal, shot him to death, when they were at once surrounded by the exasperated Indians, and a battle, short and decisive, was fought, and every man of the miners was killed, but not before twice their number of Indians had shared the same fate.

This was another sad chapter of this unholy war.

The Indians now approached the river, but, owing to the thick underbrush, were obliged to abandon all their carts,

—their ponies they took with them, but their winter's supply of meat they abandoned.

Our skirmish line was formed at three paces, but even then it was impossible to observe a line, so thick were the weeds and underbrush. The enemy was sighted, and an advance ordered, when the line moved forward, and after an hour of hard work, we, like De Soto, when he discovered the Mississippi, gazed in admiration on its prototype,—the Missouri.

After having for weeks drank the brackish water of the prairie lakes, we drank from this sweet though turbid stream, and were refreshed, as were the children of Israel, who partook of the cool water from the stricken rock.

While drinking and wading in the stream, we were fired upon from the opposite shore, although a flag of truce had been raised. The Indians' bullets fell short of their mark, but the retreat was sounded, and we marched back for the open prairie, and returned to our camp, which was situated on a beautiful plateau a few miles below. The brush was so thick that the Indians were obliged to abandon all of their carts and camp equipage, with thousands of buffalo robes, and tons of dried meat. The rout of the Indians and destruction of property was complete.

Our casualties were very light; but, among the killed was Lieutenant Beaver, an English lord, who came to this country to engage in a buffalo hunt; but, upon his arrival, learning of the Indian outbreak, tendered his services to the Government, and was commissioned a lieutenant on General Sibley's staff, as aide-de-camp. He had been sent by General Sibley with an order to Colonel Crooks, who was in command of the advance, and, on his return, he and his beautiful black horse were killed.

Colonel Crooks said to Lieutenant Beaver that the regiment would return as soon as the skirmishers could be rallied, and invited him to remain and ride with him back to camp, but the aide, true soldier that he was, felt it his duty to report to General Sibley at once, and paid the penalty.

The Indians, some at least, not being able to cross the river, were in hiding, and others had re-crossed, and were skulking in the thick brush, waiting for a chance to shoot with arrows. Lieutenant Beaver had mistaken the path he came in on, and took one that led him on to some of these skulking Indians, and he thus met his death.

Colonel Crooks returned, and though Lieutenant Beaver messed with him, his tent was at General Sibley's headquarters, and his absence from mess was not noticed until, upon inquiry at the General's tent, it was found he had not reported. The sudden disappearance of one who was such a general favorite cast a gloom over the camp.

As soon as it became dark fire rockets were sent up, in hopes that if he was wandering away, through taking a wrong road, he might be guided back to camp. The early morning found us astir, for a detail of my regiment had been made to reconnoiter and to skirmish clear down to the bank of the river, in order to gain tidings of Lieutenant Beaver, and, also, of Private Miller, of the Sixth Regiment, who also was missing.

The reconnoissance proved successful, and both bodies were found, as well as the body of the lieutenant's horse. Lieutenant Beaver had evidently made a desperate fight for his life, because his two revolvers were empty, and the indications were that he had made more than one of the enemy bite the dust.

Sighting the Enemy on the Missouri.

The bodies were brought to camp and prepared for burial in the trenches on opposite sides of the camp, and the work was so done as to obliterate all signs and prevent the Indians from locating the spots and desecrating the graves. The service was touchingly solemn, and many tears were shed, as we thought of these lonely graves so far away from the homes of the living relatives.

Lieutenant Beaver had friends in England who were abundantly able to have his remains disinterred and removed to a more suitable place of burial. Money was sent out from England for this purpose, and trusted agents sent up to the Missouri banks for the purpose of bringing back the remains. There is a grave at Graceland, in St. Paul, on the top of which rests a slab of granite, and engraven on this are the words:

"Sacred to the memory of Lieutenant F. J. H. Beaver, who died July 28, 1863. Peace to his ashes."

On the banks of the Missouri is a lonely grave. The winter's storms and the summer's heat have come and gone. The night vigils of the strange birds have been kept, the requiem of gentle breezes has been sung over this lonely grave. Comrade Nicholas Miller, private of Company K, Sixth Minnesota Infantry Volunteers, sleeps in his lonely bed, and "after life's fitful fever he sleeps well."

CHAPTER XLI.

HOMEWARD BOUND

We remained but two days at this Missouri camp, when the reveille sounded early in the morning of August 1st, and the troops were astir. We were a long way from home, and on short rations; and, in addition to this, we felt some anxiety about the boys we left at Camp Atchison, having heard nothing from them. The sun was very hot the day we left; one of the kind the boys called "muggy,"— disagreeable in the extreme. At dress parade the night before, we received the compliments of the General in orders read, announcing that the purpose of the expedition had been accomplished. This was, of course, good news to us, and we speculated as to how early a date would find us taking leave of this far-away camp.

The scouts reported to the General that Indians had been crossing the river below us all day long, and the indications were that they intended to make an attack about midnight, in order to steal our teams. With this information before him, General Sibley ordered one-half the command out on guard, and the balance to lay on their arms. In an hour or so another order came, for the balance of the command to reinforce the guard, because there surely would be an attack, and it did come about twelve o'clock;

MINNESOTA MASSACRE—1862. 253

but the attempt to capture the teams miscarried; for, after a few shots, the Indians retired. Having lost nearly all of their wagons and cured meat, they were in a desperate condition, and a commissary train would have been a rich prize.

On the morning we left it was astonishing how quickly we got ready, and how lonesome the canvas city looked after the bugle sounded "strike tents." We marched out this fine morning with our banners flying, and the band playing "The Girl I Left Behind Me."

There were no regrets, for the "beautiful Indian maiden" had not made a favorable impression on us, and we had our own little families at home.

The Sixth Minnesota was in the rear, and we were hardly beyond the limits of the camp before the Indians had taken possession and commenced firing on our rear guard. The Colonel gave the necessary commands to bring us to a "right about," with orders to "commence firing." The orders came in quick succession, and were such a surprise to the Indians that they took to their heels with great alacrity. They hovered about us during all the day, but did not in the least retard us in our homeward march. We were instructed to supply ourselves with water before starting, because we must march eighteen miles, to Apple river bend, before we could get a fresh supply.

The day was excessively warm, and the men became thirsty; but, behold! we look away, and a beautiful lake appears before us. "Water! water!" cry the thirsty men, and our canteens were soon empty, in anticipation of refilling them from the bosom of this beautiful lake before us. We march and thirst again, and the beautiful lake seems just as far away.

"It's two miles to that lake," says one thirsty soul. We march the two miles, and yet are two miles away, and the thirst and heat are intolerable.

"Surely that's water," said another, "but we don't seem to get any nearer to it."

We marched and marched; but we must be in a valley, for the lake is out of sight.

"When we get over the ridge we'll see the beautiful lake," comes from some one in the ranks.

We got over the ridge, but the beautiful lake, in all its refreshing loveliness, had vanished. Had it evaporated, or had it sunk into the ground? Neither. We had been deceived,—it was a mirage! The air was hot, the earth parched, the throats dry, the canteens empty, and we were yet eight miles from water.

Eight long, weary miles to go before we reach the bend in Apple river, but there was no help for it, and we bear to it with our soldier load. "Five miles farther," says the scout, and our hearts almost stop beating, we are so parched; three miles, and on we march; only one mile more, and we would run if we could. We reach the bank, and the Colonel commands: "Battalion, halt!" but the refreshing water is too near, and the famishing men make a run for it, and do not stop until they are in waist deep, and then they drink to their fill and replenish their canteens.

On our return march we passed nearly over the same ground as we did going out. We passed the battlefield of the Big Mound, and went into camp by the lake where Lieutenant Freeman was killed; this was on the 4th of August. The next day our scouts reported "Indians ahead,"—a false alarm,—the Indians espied were half-breeds bringing us mail from Camp Atchison, and also the news that George A. Brackett, who was with Lieutenant Freeman when he was killed, had made his way, after weary days and nights of wandering, and in a half-starved condition, to Camp Atchison, where he fell among friends.

When we arrived at Camp Atchison it took but a day to arrange for our final departure. Lieutenant Freeman's body had been recovered and buried, and the place so marked that it was easily found afterwards, when the body was removed and taken to his home for final interment.

We drew five days' rations of hard tack and bacon, and the side dishes that go with it; just what they were I cannot now remember. I guess the dear old army bean was one and desiccated vegetable another; anyway, we were not troubled with the gout from too much eating of rich food. The surgeons made proper provision for the transportation of the sick by placing them in ambulances, and at an early hour the headquarters' bugler sounded "strike tents," and the canvas city was razed to the ground; —Camp Atchison was a back number.

The command took up the line of march for Fort Snelling, where we expected to receive orders to proceed at once to join the Union Army in the South. We were a jolly crowd, and the march seemed but a pleasant pastime; we had driven the enemy out of the country, and, save the first two or three days of our return march, he was giving us no trouble. We made good time, and the nearer we got home the shorter the miles became.

When we got down to civilization we were accorded an ovation; especially was this the case at Minneapolis, where the whole city turned out to bid us welcome.

We arrived at Fort Snelling on the morning of September 12th, after having made a march of more than twelve hundred miles;—and thus ended the campaign of 1863.

CHAPTER XLII.

THE CAMPAIGN OF 1864.

My active work in the Sioux Indian war ended in the autumn of 1863, and the regiment went South, but history has made me familiar with the campaign of 1864, and I thus devote space to it, so as to follow the troops and Indians to the culmination and final successful closing of the greatest Indian war of modern times.

The return of General Sibley from the Missouri campaign of 1863 did not end the Sioux war, because, while the Indians had been defeated in five pitched battles in 1862 and '63, yet they were known to be in large numbers, ready to take the field again in 1864, as soon as the weather would permit. Such being the case, it became necessary to organize against them.

To this end another expedition was fitted out from the Minnesota side, which was to co-operate with General Sully from the Missouri side. General Sully, on account of the low stage of water in the Missouri in 1863, was unable to co-operate with General Sibley, as was intended, and on August 1st, 1863, and when General Sibley's order for the homeward march was promulgated, General Sully was one hundred and sixty miles farther down the river than it was intended he should be. This was the reason why the Indians were not more severely whipped than they were. It would have been suicidal for General Sibley to have crossed the Missouri river at this time, with rations and ammunition as scarce as they were.

The Indians took advantage of the situation and evinced a determination to take the field again. A cavalry regiment had been authorized by the War Department for one year and for frontier service. This regiment was filled to the maximum, and placed in command of Colonel R. N. McLaren.

A battalion had been raised previous to this, known as Hatch's battalion, and was on duty near Pembina, and by this wise provision confidence was restored in this part of the country.

The Indians still had undisputed possession of the country west of the Missouri, and, although they may have been peaceable, it was necessary to settle the question permanently, and place them on their reservations.

The plan of the campaign of 1864 was very similar to that of the year previous, excepting in the matter of command, the two columns,—the one from the Minnesota side and the other from the Missouri side,—were to combine and become two brigades, under the command of General Sully.

The first brigade was composed of Iowa and Kansas infantry, and they embarked at Sioux City, Iowa, and proceeded up the Missouri. The second brigade embraced the Eighth Minnesota Infantry, mounted on ponies, Colonel M. T. Thomas in command; the Second Minnesota Cavalry, Colonel McLaren; and the Third Minnesota Battery, Captain John Jones. This brigade was in command of Colonel Thomas, and left Fort Snelling on June 1st.

General Sibley and staff accompanied this brigade of 2,100 men as far as Fort Ridgely, where he gave them their final orders.

Colonel Thomas, who considered General Sibley a man of ability, thought him too cautious, and, in response to his final orders, said: "General, I am going to hunt for Indians; if they will hunt for and find me it will save a heap of trouble."

It was a beautiful morning on June 5th, and as the first rays of the morning sun flashed the full light of day, "boots and saddles" sounded in the clear tones of the bugles, and the column, headed by a magnificent band, mounted on milk white horses, marched out to the tune of "The Girl I Left Behind Me."

The General reviewed the column as it passed, and after complimenting the appearance of the soldiers and bidding good-bye to Colonel Thomas and his staff, who were starting on a five months' campaign beyond the bounds of civilization, rode back to the fort.

The column was now under way, and day after day the march went on, in solid square, so organized that all the Indians in North America could not disturb it. At night the square closed up, so as to ensure greater safety and reduce guard duty.

The column moved up the valley of the Minnesota river to its source, and then took a westerly course, making daily from sixteen to twenty miles, resting on Sunday.

The scouts, failing to find even signs of Indians, the march became monotonous until the valley of the Missouri was reached. Here was found General Sully's trail of the year previous, and soon some of his scouts came into camp and reported General Sully only one day's march away, where he was waiting for the fleet of boats on which were supplies for the troops.

The monotony of the daily march was enlivened by the report that Indians were hovering around,—they came to reconnoiter, but not to fight yet. This of itself was encouraging, because the boys began to think they would not even see an Indian; but there was fun ahead, as we shall see in the next chapter.

CHAPTER XLIII.

THE BATTLE OF THE BAD LANDS.

General Sully, an unpretentious man, with clear perception, appeared to know where the Indians were, and what they would do. His service in the regular army peculiarly fitted him for this service, and this, with his genial temperament, made him an agreeable commander.

The boats were unloaded, the command supplied with sixty days' rations and divested of all surplus clothing and equipments, made ready for a vigorous march after Indians.

The troops were reviewed by the commanding officer, General Sully, who, by the way, was at one time Colonel of the First Minnesota, and afterwards promoted to Major-General of Volunteers and Brevet Brigadier-General of the regular army. The review of the troops constituted the celebrating the Fourth of July, 1864.

When the column finally moved, which was on July 19, it marched out into an unknown and unexplored country, from the white man's standpoint.

What a transformation,—then unknown and unexplored, —no highways, no railroads, no civilization,—to-day the onward march of our race has left its imprint by railroads, beautiful farms, busy cities, busy factories, Christian civili-

RESTING BEFORE AN ATTACK.

zation, education and the "little red school house." But I am anticipating; turn back the leaves and we are again on the Knife river, and we snuff a battle, for the Indians are ahead in great numbers.

It was on July 28th, among the foothills of the mountains, that a large camp of Indians was found. In this camp were no less than one hundred and ten bands of hostile Sioux, and they meant business, for they had congregated here for the express purpose of cleaning out the white soldiers, and they felt confident they could do it.

The Indians, on their horses, were stripped for the fray, and began leisurely to ride in line of battle toward the white enemy. When within rifle shot, the soldiers opened fire, and instantly the scene was changed. The bands concentrated, and, uttering their war cries, they dashed at full speed on our lines, firing, and, like the wind, whirled to the rear, loading as they went, when they would again face the enemy, and, coming within gunshot, fire again.

They were so confident of success that they did not attempt to save their own camp, which was the objective point of the soldiers; and they did not realize their dangerous position until they found that their terrific onslaught on our lines did not in the least impede the progress of the troops.

Soon the artillery was brought up, and the shells were sent thick and fast among them. By this time they began to realize that retreat were the tactics now.

There were 1,600 tepees filled with women and children, with the usual supply of dogs,—not less than two dogs to a tepee, and such a stampede.

It was a grand sight in one sense and sad in another. To see this great, moving mass of 10,000 or 12,000 souls, with their camp paraphernalia, including dogs and ponies, rushing over the prairie; the fleeing multitude spread out as far as the eye could reach on either side, rushing on in mad haste, as though fleeing from the city of destruction. It was the sight of a lifetime, but sad to contemplate that the sins of some were being showered upon the heads of the innocent women and children.

The loss to the Indians in killed was estimated at 100 to 150; the wounded they carried off the field. The dead were buried in the night in large trenches, the earth leveled off, and the troops marched away.

The Indians were not satisfied with the result of this engagement; they naturally would not be. They claimed that the best of their young men were off hunting for our troops in another direction, and they should at once call them in and give battle again.

The last six days had been very exciting, and was a nervous strain on the soldiers. One hundred and seventy-five miles had been made, a battle of eight hours had been fought, and the camp of Indians destroyed.

The march to the west was resumed over the prairie, with the Knife Mountains to the north and the Black Hills to the south, looming up in the distance like great sentinels, standing to contest the approach of civilization and defying the elements of ages.

In the immediate front, off towards the horizon, was what seemed to be a level plain,—it was level, but for a little distance, and then broke to your view what might have inspired a Dante to write a more recent edition of Inferno; for, as far as the eye could reach, north and south and for forty miles to the west, the body of the earth had been rent and torn asunder, as though giant demons, in their infuriated defeat, had sought to disembowel the earth.

General Sully said of it: "It is hell with the fires put out."

We are now in the Bad Lands, and it is Sunday,—the Lord's day, and in such a region,—where devils had fought. White men's eyes had probably never before seen this region, and the Indians were afraid of it; they looked upon this region as the abode of evil spirits, and that the great gorges and buttes and yawning chasms were but the product of their wrath.

The Sunday passed quietly until after noon, when a reconnoitering party returned and said they had been fired upon by Indians.

About five o'clock on this Sunday General Sully changed the position of the camp and went four miles farther up the river, in order to be in better position to prevent a surprise or repel an attack.

The Indians were interested observers, for while this move was being made 1,000 of them were quietly sitting on their horses on the surrounding hills, observing.

General Sully, being sick in his tent at this time, the command devolved upon Colonel Thomas, of the Eighth Minnesota, and to him he gave orders to "have everything ready to move at six o'clock in the morning, in perfect fighting order; put one of your most active field officers in charge of a strong advance guard, and you will meet them at the head of the ravine, and have the biggest Indian fight that ever will happen on this continent; and let me further say that under no circumstances must any man turn his back on a live Indian."

On Monday morning, bright and early, on August 8th,

1864, the columns were formed. The General was in an ambulance at the front, and in admiration looking up and down the lines of the soldiers who were so soon to engage the Indians in battle, gave vent to his feelings in words more expressive than elegant: "Those fellows can whip the devil and all his angels."

General Sully himself was unable to go farther, but when he grasped Colonel Thomas, who was in immediate command, by the hand he said: "You must make some history to-day."

"Forward!" and the column is marching out, and not a sound is there to indicate that its progress will be impeded, as we enter the narrow gorge, only wide enough for a wagon trail. Almost an hour passes in steadily climbing up the narrow and secluded way, and when near the head of the gulch, from the beautiful stillness of the morning the pandemonium of war broke loose.

The artillery advanced in a gallop, and, in position, soon commenced planting shells among the redskins. This was followed up by the steady advance of the dismounted men, who pressed their lines, and they commenced to fall back. The General, sick though he was, and in the ambulance, could not endure being there when the fight was going on, so he ordered up his horse and, mounting, rode to the front, but nature resisted, and he was obliged to dismount, which he did, and seating himself on a boulder, with his field glass took in the whole situation. Colonel Thomas, who was in command, hearing that the General was on the field, sought him out and said: "I am ready to advance, sir."

The General, pointing his hand toward a range of hills, said: "Go ahead, you will find the camp beyond those buttes; hold your men well in hand, push the Indians;

they will fight for their families; protect your flank, and I will protect the rear."

The fight went on; the wounded were sent to the rear, and for twelve miles we drove the Indians from point to point, but darkness came on before their camp was reached.

In the bivouac at night the scene was a varied one. At the roll-call there were names not answered, for the unerring arrow and Indian bullet had done its work. At the next muster it would be necessary to mark after some name: "Killed in battle in the Bad Lands August 8th, 1864," or, "died of wounds received from Indians in battle in the Bad Lands August 8th, 1864," for there were 109 killed and wounded on this day.

The wounded received proper attention at once, and the other soldiers, well tired out with the day's fighting and marching, were soundly sleeping and dreaming of home.

There were 8,000 warriors engaged in this battle, and as nearly as could be estimated they lost 350 killed and from 600 to 800 wounded. It was a bloody battle, and the field was named by the Indians Waps-chon-choka.

The Indians, after this decisive battle, broke up into small bands and went in every direction, so that the soldiers, as an army, could not well follow them.

The war had ended so far as the Indians were concerned, but there was another fight on hand. Bad water and lack of rations are not a happy condition of affairs, and the soldiers had to look this square in the face. And hot! The tongues of some of the men were so swelled from thirst and heat that they could not talk. The animals suffered equally with the men, and in numerous instances it became necessary to put them out of their misery by blowing out their brains.

And thus things went on from day to day until August 12th, when glad news came from one of the scouts, who came riding back and frantically waving something in his hands. It was simply a little chip of wood, and why should this create such unbounded joy among a lot of war-begrimed veterans? It was freshly cut and evidently came from the steamboat men, as it was borne down on the bosom of the cool waters of the longed-for Yellowstone.

The weary soldiers, thirsting and starving, viewed this little harbinger of plenty with delight, and their strength began to return as they increased their step in the march toward the river.

O, that beautiful river:—"The Nectar of the Gods." How life-inspiring its fluid, as discipline was forgotten and joy and happy shouts took the place of misery in the command.

The thirst was slaked, and now for something to eat, for soldiers, poor mortals, get very hungry, and how often they longed for some good home-made bread and sugar and cream for coffee. And pies; well, our mouths used to fairly water for pies. But, on this especial occasion, almost anything would do, for the boys were awfully hungry, and the commissary was like "Old Mother Hubbard's" cupboard—empty.

There were timber bottoms a little way down the river full of elk and black-tailed deer, so the Indians informed us.

A detail was made, and the hunters went out in search of game, and before night they returned with the evidence of their day's hunt with them. They were like the spies sent out in Bible times, who came back laden with grapes, and reported that the country which they had explored was rich, and flowed with milk and honey.

So, too, our soldier-hunters said the bottom lands were alive with elk and deer; and, by the next night, the luscious ribs and steaks were sizzling in the blaze, and hunger was being appeased as well as the thirst had been.

The war being practically over, the several commands returned by various routes to the points from whence they came, and were at once ordered South to take their places in some of the other armies. The campaigns of 1862, '63 and '64 were successfully carried out, and we will recapitulate our desires, our journeyings, our hopes and our fears and our rejoicings in another chapter, and bid you adieu.

EXAMINING THE COLORS AFTER THE CAMPAIGN.

CHAPTER XLIV.

CONCLUSION.

In writing this narrative my mind has been refreshed and incidents and the names of persons almost forgotten come to me—they press on my memory.

I am able to recall many, but to specify them would unduly lengthen this book. There was one important character, however, whom I had quite forgotten at the proper time, and in this concluding chapter must make mention of him.

Pierre Bottineau came originally from the Selkirk settlement, and in 1837 made a claim near St. Anthony Falls.

I was with him upon the plains of Dakota in 1857, and in his way he was a remarkable man. On one occasion the party got lost in a furious storm and we knew that war parties of Chippewas were roaming over the prairie and it was not any way too healthy to be in the region we supposed we were wandering in. We halted to hold a council and Pierre said: "As soon as the stars come out I can locate." So we waited and waited for the storm to pass over. The night was pitchy dark, but in time the stars came, when Pierre laid flat down on the ground, face up, and for perhaps half an hour surveyed the heavens and located our wandering feet. We were soon on the right trail for our camp, which was forty or fifty miles away.

Pierre was one of General Sibley's principal scouts during the several campaigns against the Indians in 1862 and 1863. He died some years ago, and speaking of his death reminds me of others prominent in these military operations who have gone beyond the river.

The two generals, Sibley and Sully, are gone, and of the field and staff, I can recall Colonel John T. Averill, of the Sixth Minnesota, who was, after the war, member of Congress. Adjutant Snow and Quartermasters Carver and Gilbert, Colonels Stephen Miller and Wm. R. Marshall, both honored by Minnesota by electing them to chief executive—they, with Lieut. Colonel Bradley and all of the Seventh; Colonel Robert N. McLaren, of the Second Cavalry, and Major Hatch, of the battalion bearing his name, and Captain John Jones, of the famous battery. These are among some of the chiefs who have been called.

Among the line of officers and the rank and file, it

would be a mighty host, and it saddens my heart when I think of them, so I will desist and conclude by reminding you of the invitation extended and briefly recapitulate our journeyings.

READER: The invitation extended to you to accompany us on a military expedition into the Indian country has been accepted. It was under exciting circumstances, when the whole country was surcharged with alarm, and for good cause.

The Indians, cruel, relentless, revengeful, and with determination, were murdering innocent men, women and children, and but for the friendly offices of a faithful few, whose hearts were whiter than their skins, the death list and list of horrors would have been far greater; and it is for these few we speak when we say there are good Indians other than dead ones; and Minnesota could not do a more appropriate thing to-day than erect a monument to the memory of Old Betz, Other Day, Shaska and others, who risked their lives to save their white friends from the tomahawk of their more vengeful brethren, and who did so much to alleviate the sufferings and to relieve the anxiety of the captive prisoners.

You went with us to besieged New Ulm and Fort Ridgely; helped bury the dead at Redwood; marched with us and went into camp and endured the thirty-six hours of anxiety and suffering at Birch Coolie; helped bury the dead and care for the wounded there; returned with us to Fort Ridgely; took part in the battle at Wood Lake, where the Indians were defeated; shared our joys when we liberated the women at Camp Release; helped arrest, shackle and guard the Indians; witnessed the execution of thirty-eight at Mankato; marched across with the "Moscow Expedition"; rendezvoused with us at Camp Pope in 1863; marched and fought Indians with us at Big Mound, Dead Buffalo Lake, Stony Lake and the Missouri River. You mingled your tears with ours over Beaver's and Miller's graves, as we left them in their loneliness on the bank of the river; participated in and rejoiced with us all the way on our return, took part in the campaign of 1864, and now, before bidding you adieu, one question: Are you satisfied?

THE END.

www.ingramcontent.com/pod-product-compliance
Lightning Source LLC
Chambersburg PA
CBHW031954230426
43672CB00010B/2151